W9-AXV-071

Japanese Phrases
FOR
DUMMIES®

by Eriko Sato, PhD

WILEY

Wiley Publishing, Inc.

Japanese Phrases For Dummies®

Published by
Wiley Publishing, Inc.
111 River St.
Hoboken, NJ 07030-5774
www.wiley.com

Copyright © 2004 by Wiley Publishing, Inc., Indianapolis, Indiana

Published by Wiley Publishing, Inc., Indianapolis, Indiana

Published simultaneously in Canada

No part of this publication may be reproduced, stored in a retrieval system, or trans-mitted in any form or by any means, electronic, mechanical, photocopying, recording, scanning, or otherwise, except as permitted under Sections 107 or 108 of the 1976 United States Copyright Act, without either the prior written permission of the Publisher, or authorization through payment of the appropriate per-copy fee to the Copyright Clearance Center, 222 Rosewood Drive, Danvers, MA 01923, 978-750-8400, fax 978-646-8600. Requests to the Publisher for permission should be addressed to the Legal Department, Wiley Publishing, Inc., 10475 Crosspoint Blvd., Indianapolis, IN 46256, 317-572-3447, fax 317-572-4355, or e-mail brandreview@wiley.com.

Trademarks: Wiley, the Wiley Publishing logo, For Dummies, the Dummies Man logo, A Reference for the Rest of Us!, The Dummies Way, Dummies Daily, The Fun and Easy Way, Dummies.com and related trade dress are trademarks or registered trademarks of John Wiley & Sons, Inc. and/or its affiliates in the United States and other countries, and may not be used without written permission. All other trademarks are the prop-erty of their respective owners. Wiley Publishing, Inc., is not associated with any prod-uct or vendor mentioned in this book.

LIMIT OF LIABILITY/DISCLAIMER OF WARRANTY: THE PUBLISHER AND THE AUTHOR MAKE NO REPRESENTATIONS OR WARRANTIES WITH RESPECT TO THE ACCURACY OR COMPLETENESS OF THE CONTENTS OF THIS WORK AND SPECIFICALLY DISCLAIM ALL WARRANTIES, INCLUDING WITHOUT LIMITATION WARRANTIES OF FITNESS FOR A PARTICULAR PURPOSE. NO WARRANTY MAY BE CREATED OR EXTENDED BY SALES OR PROMOTIONAL MATERIALS. THE ADVICE AND STRATEGIES CONTAINED HEREIN MAY NOT BE SUITABLE FOR EVERY SITUATION. THIS WORK IS SOLD WITH THE UNDERSTANDING THAT THE PUBLISHER IS NOT ENGAGED IN RENDERING LEGAL, ACCOUNTING, OR OTHER PROFESSIONAL SERVICES. IF PROFESSIONAL ASSISTANCE IS REQUIRED, THE SERVICES OF A COMPETENT PROFESSIONAL PERSON SHOULD BE SOUGHT. NEITHER THE PUBLISHER NOR THE AUTHOR SHALL BE LIABLE FOR DAMAGES ARISING HERE-FROM. THE FACT THAT AN ORGANIZATION OR WEBSITE IS REFERRED TO IN THIS WORK AS A CITATION AND/OR A POTENTIAL SOURCE OF FURTHER INFORMATION DOES NOT MEAN THAT THE AUTHOR OR THE PUBLISHER ENDORSES THE INFORMATION THE ORGANIZATION OR WEBSITE MAY PROVIDE OR RECOMMENDATIONS IT MAY MAKE. FURTHER, READERS SHOULD BE AWARE THAT INTERNET WEBSITES LISTED IN THIS WORK MAY HAVE CHANGED OR DISAP-PEARED BETWEEN WHEN THIS WORK WAS WRITTEN AND WHEN IT IS READ.

For general information on our other products and services or to obtain technical support, please contact our Customer Care Department within the U.S. at 800-762-2974, outside the U.S. at 317-572-3993, or fax 317-572-4002.

Wiley also publishes its books in a variety of electronic formats. Some content that appears in print may not be available in electronic books.

Library of Congress Control Number: 2004108052

ISBN: 0-7645-7205-9

Manufactured in the United States of America

10   9   8   7   6

1O/RZ/QX/QU/IN

About the Authors

Eriko Sato is a lecturer of Japanese language at the State University of New York at Stony Brook, where she received her PhD degree in linguistics. She also is the Founding Director of the Pre-College Japanese Language Program as well as the Executive Director of the Japan Center at the same university. When she started her graduate work in 1988, she decided to devote her career to Japanese-language education and research. She studied Japanese and English linguistics and foreign languages, including Chinese, French, and Korean, to prepare herself to be a teacher and researcher who understands students' linguistic backgrounds and difficulties. She has written many articles for linguistic and education journals, and she has written three books on Japanese language: a textbook for young children, a textbook for college students, and a manual for Japanese/English translators.

Publisher's Acknowledgments

We're proud of this book; please send us your comments through our Dummies online registration form located at www.dummies.com/register/.

Some of the people who helped bring this book to market include the following:

Acquisitions, Editorial, and Media Development

Compilation Editor:
Pam Mourouzis

Senior Project Editor:
Alissa Schwipps

Acquisitions Editor:
Stacy Kennedy

Copy Editor: Michelle Dzurny

Technical Editor:
Susan Furukawa

Editorial Manager:
Jennifer Ehrlich

Editorial Assistants:
Courtney Allen,
Melissa Bennett

Cartoons: Rich Tennant,
www.the5thwave.com

Composition

Project Coordinator:
Nancee Reeves

Layout and Graphics:
Michael Kruzil,
Heather Ryan,
Jacque Schneider,
Julie Trippetti

Proofreaders: Kyle Looper,
Brian H. Walls

Indexer: Tom Dinse

Publishing and Editorial for Consumer Dummies

Diane Graves Steele, Vice President and Publisher,
Consumer Dummies

Joyce Pepple, Acquisitions Director, Consumer Dummies

Kristin A. Cocks, Product Development Director,
Consumer Dummies

Michael Spring, Vice President and Publisher, Travel

Brice Gosnell, Associate Publisher, Travel

Kelly Regan, Editorial Director, Travel

Publishing for Technology Dummies

Andy Cummings, Vice President and Publisher, Dummies
Technology/General User

Composition Services

Gerry Fahey, Vice President of Production Services

Debbie Stailey, Director of Composition Services

Table of Contents

• •

Introduction

∎∎∎∎∎∎∎∎∎∎∎∎∎∎∎∎∎∎∎∎∎∎∎∎∎∎∎∎∎∎∎∎∎

Exchanging ideas and friendships across national
and cultural boundaries are the keys to making
our lives richer and more meaningful. And traveling
abroad is a lot cheaper than it used to be. Grabbing
your passport and setting off on an adventure is
always fun, but it's even more fun when you can communicate with people in a different country in their
native language.

If you want to learn a little Japanese, this book can
help. It provides instant results in the form of key
words and phrases that a beginning speaker is likely
to want to know, plus some cultural background. You
won't become fluent by reading *Japanese Phrases For
Dummies,* but you will gain confidence, have fun, and
pick up some Japanese sayings that you can put to
good use.

About This Book

Japanese Phrases For Dummies can help you whether
you're planning a trip to Japan, dealing with Japanese
companies at work, or wanting to say good morning
to your new neighbor who's Japanese. [Try **ohayō
gozaimasu** (oh-hah-yohh goh-zah-ee-mah-soo; good
morning).] This book gives you the most important
and most-used Japanese words and phrases on subjects as diverse as shopping, money, food, and leisure
activities.

You can read as much or as little of this book as you
like. Decide what topic you're interested in, consult the
index or the table of contents, and you'll quickly find
the information that you need. If you're unfamiliar with
Japanese, I highly recommend reading Chapters 1 and 2

first because they contain the basics of Japanese pronunciation and grammar. If you're already familiar with Japanese, you can always refer to these chapters if you get hung up on a pronunciation or grammar issue.

Conventions Used in This Book

I use a few conventions in this book to help your reading go smoothly:

- ✔ All vowels and consonants are in **rōmaji** (rohh-mah-jee; Roman letters) so you see the familiar English alphabet. The Japanese use their own system called **kana** (kah-nah) and about 2,000 Chinese characters in their daily lives, but they also use **rōmaji** for the convenience of foreigners.

- ✔ A straight bar (ˉ) over a vowel indicates *a long vowel,* which means you draw out the sound.

- ✔ Japanese terms stand out in **boldface** type.

- ✔ In the parentheses that follow Japanese terms, the pronunciations are first and the English translation is second. For example, **Dōmo** (dohh-moh; Thank you *or* Hi!).

- ✔ I write *verb conjugations* (lists that show the basic forms of a verb; see Chapter 2) in tables in this order: the dictionary form, the negative form, the stem form, and the te-form. Here's an example of a verb table using the verb **taberu** (tah-beh-roo; to eat):

Conjugation	*Pronunciation*
taberu	tah-beh-roo
tabenai	tah-beh-nah-ee
tabe	tah-beh
tabete	tah-beh-teh

✔ The black boxes highlight the key words and phrases in the section or chapter. When I list an adjective, I list na-type adjectives in the stem form without the **na** and i-type adjectives in the stem form plus the inflection **i.** I do this because **i** appears almost all the time, but **na** appears only when the adjective is followed by a noun.

Different languages express the same ideas differently. English and Japanese are no exception. Japanese has many words and phrases that can't be translated into English. In this book, I want you to know *what* is said (the intended meaning) rather than *how* it's said. Instead of giving literal translations, I give natural English translations. For example, the phrase **yoroshiku** (yoh-roh-shee-koo) literally translates as "appropriately," but the phrase really means "pleased to meet you" if you say it when you meet someone new.

The way I translate Japanese phrases and sentences can differ depending on the context. For example, I may translate **yoroshiku** as "thanks for doing me a favor" instead of "pleased to meet you" if it's used right after asking a favor of someone.

Foolish Assumptions

To write this book, I made some assumptions about you, the reader:

✔ You don't know much Japanese, except maybe a few words like **karate** and **sushi.**

✔ You know some Japanese, but you'd like a refresher.

✔ You aren't taking a Japanese language proficiency test next month and you aren't planning on becoming a Japanese translator in the near future. You just want to be able to communicate basic information in Japanese.

> ✔ You don't have hours to spend memorizing vocabulary words and grammar rules.

> ✔ You want to have fun in addition to acquiring a little Japanese.

If these assumptions apply to you, you're in business!

Icons Used in This Book

To alert you to important points, I placed some icons in the margins throughout this book. They help you find certain types of information quickly. Here's what the icons mean:

This icon highlights tips that can make picking up Japanese easier.

To ensure that you don't forget an important piece of information, this icon serves as a reminder.

This icon points out discussions of odd grammar rules.

If you're interested in cultural and travel-related information, look for this icon. It draws your attention to interesting tidbits about Japan and the Japanese culture.

Where to Go from Here

The most important step in speaking a language is to use the words and phrases that you learn. So read about the topics that interest you and then make sure to use your favorite Japanese phrases while hanging out with your friends and family. If you follow this plan, you'll be able to answer **Hai** (hah-ee; Yes!) confidently when people ask **Nihongo wa hanasemasu ka** (nee-hohn-goh wah hah-nah-seh-mah-soo kah; Can you speak Japanese?).

Chapter 1

I Say It How? Speaking Japanese

In This Chapter

▶ Getting the basic sounds down

▶ Recognizing the Japanese you already know

▶ Perfecting some phrases

*F*iguring out how to speak a foreign language is a great way to explore a different culture. In this chapter, you open your mouth and sound like a totally different person — a Japanese-speaking person! I tell you how to say familiar Japanese words (like **sushi**) with an authentic Japanese accent. **Jā, hajimemashō** (jahh, hah-jee-meh-mah-shohh; Let's start!).

Basic Japanese Sounds

Japanese sounds are easy to hear and pronounce. Each syllable is simple, short, and usually enunciated very clearly. With a little practice, you'll get use to them quickly. This section gets you off on the right foot (or should I say the right sound) by looking at vowels, consonants, and a couple of letter combinations.

Vowel sounds

Japanese has only five basic vowels — *a, e, i, o,* and *u* — all of which sound short and crisp — plus their longer counterparts, *ā, ē, ī, ō,* and *ū.*

Short and long vowel sounds in Japanese are quite different than they are in English. In Japanese, long vowels have the same sounds as short vowels — you just draw out the sounds for a moment longer. To an English-speaking ear, a long Japanese vowel sounds as if it's being stressed.

Whether a vowel is long or short can make all the difference in the meaning of a Japanese word. For example, **obasan** (oh-bah-sahn) with a short *a* means "aunt," but **obāsan** (oh-bahh-sahn) with a long *ā* means "grand-mother." If you don't differentiate the vowel length properly, no one will understand who you're talking about.

Table 1-1 lists the Japanese vowels. Practice saying them a few times to get the hang of how they sound.

Table 1-1		Japanese Vowel Sounds	
Letter	*Pronunciation*	*English Word with the Sound*	*Example*
a	ah	a<u>ha</u>	obasan (oh-bah-sahn; aunt)
ā	ahh		obāsan (oh-bahh-sahn; grandmother)
e	eh	b<u>e</u>d	Seto (seh-toh; a city in Japan)
ē	ehh		sēto (sehh-toh; pupil)
i	ee	f<u>ee</u>t	ojisan (oh-jee-sahn; uncle)

Letter	Pronunciation	English Word with the Sound	Example
ī or ii	eee		ojīsan (oh-jeee-sahn; grandfather
o	oh	d<u>o</u>me	tori (toh-ree; bird)
ō	ohh		tōri (tohh-ree; street)
u	oo	f<u>oo</u>t	yuki (yoo-kee; snow)
ū	ooo		yūki (yooo-kee; courage)

In Japanese, any two vowels can appear next to each other in a word. You may hear them as one vowel sound, but to the Japanese, they sound like two vowels. For example, **ai** (ah-ee; love) sounds like one vowel — the English *i* (as in *eye*) — but to the Japanese, it's actually two vowels, not one. The word **koi** (koh-ee; carp) sounds like the one-syllable English word *coy*, but in Japanese, **koi** is a two-syllable word.

Table 1-2 lists some other common vowel combinations. Some of them may sound awfully similar to you, but Japanese speakers hear them differently. Try saying them aloud so that you can hear the differences.

Table 1-2	Vowel Combinations	
Vowel Combination	*Pronunciation*	*Translation*
ai	ah-ee	love
mae	mah-eh	front
ao	ah-oh	blue
au	ah-oo	meet
ue	oo-eh	up
koi	koh-ee	carp
koe	koh-eh	voice

The vowels *i* (ee) and *u* (oo) come out as a whisper whenever they fall between the consonant sounds *ch, h, k, p, s, sh, t,* and *ts* or whenever a word ends in this consonant-vowel combination. What do those consonants have in common? They're what linguists call "voiceless," meaning that they don't make your vocal cords vibrate. Put your hand over your vocal cords and say a voiceless consonant like the *k* sound. Then say a "voiced" consonant like the *g* sound. Feel the difference? Tables 1-3 and 1-4 provide examples with and without the whispered vowels.

Table 1-3	Words with Whispered Vowels	
Japanese	*Pronunciation*	*Translation*
sukēto	skehh-to	skating
kusai	ksah-ee	stinky
ashita	ah-shtah	tomorrow
sō desu	sohh dehs	that's right

Table 1-4	Words without Whispered Vowels	
Japanese	*Pronunciation*	*Translation*
sugoi	soo-goh-ee	amazing; wow
kuni	koo-nee	country
kagu	kah-goo	furniture

Consonant sounds

Fortunately, most Japanese consonants are pronounced as they are in English. Table 1-5 describes the sounds that you need to pay attention to.

Table 1-5	Japanese Consonants That Are Different from English	
Consonant	**Description of the Sound**	**Examples**
r	Here you tap your tongue on the roof of your mouth just once — almost like an English *d* or *l*, but not quite.	rakuda (rah-koo-dah; camel); tora (toh-rah; tiger); tori (toh-ree; bird)
f	A much softer sound than the English *f* — somewhere between an *f* and an *h* sound. Make the sound by bringing your lips close to each other and gently blowing air through them.	Fujisan (foo-jee-sahn; Mt. Fuji); tōfu (tohh-foo; bean curd); fūfu (fooo-foo; married couple)
ts	The combination is hard to pronounce at the beginning of a word, as in **tsunami**, although it's easy anywhere else. Try saying the word **cats** in your head and then saying **tsunami**.	tsunami (tsoo-nah-mee; tidal wave); tsuki (tsoo-kee; the moon)
ry	The combination of *r* and *y* is difficult to pronounce when it occurs before the vowel *o*. Try saying **ri** (ree) and then **yo** (yoh). Repeat many times and gradually increase the speed until you can pronounce the two sounds simultaneously. Remember that the *r* sounds almost like a *d* in English.	ryō (ryohh; dormitory); ryokan (ryoh-kahn; Japanese-style inn)

Like most other languages, Japanese has double consonants. You pronounce these double consonants — *pp, tt, kk,* and *ss* — as single consonants preceded by a brief pause. Check out the following examples:

- ✔ **kekkon** (kehk-kohn; marriage)
- ✔ **kippu** (keep-poo; tickets)
- ✔ **kitte** (keet-teh; stamps)
- ✔ **massugu** (mahs-soo-goo; straight)

Sounding Fluent

If you want to sound like a native Japanese speaker, you need to imitate the intonations, rhythms, and accents of Japanese. These almost musical aspects of the language make a big difference, and they're not that difficult to achieve.

Don't stress

English sentences sound like they're full of punches because they contain words that have stressed syllables followed by unstressed syllables. Japanese sentences sound flat because Japanese words and phrases don't have stressed syllables. So unless you're angry or excited, suppress your desire to stress syllables when you speak Japanese.

Get in rhythm

English sentences sound smooth and connected, but Japanese sentences sound choppy because each syllable is pronounced separately. You can sound like a native speaker by pronouncing each syllable separately, not connecting them as you do in English.

Pitch perfectly

Although Japanese speakers don't stress syllables, they may raise or lower the *pitch* on a specific syllable in a certain word. A raised pitch may sound like a stress, but if you think in terms of music, the high notes aren't necessarily stressed more than the low notes.

Pitch differences in Japanese are a lot subtler than the differences between musical notes. Sometimes a slight pitch difference changes the meaning of a word.

The pitch also depends on what part of Japan you're in. For example, in eastern Japan, the word **hashi** (hah-shee) means "chopsticks" when said with high-to-low pitch, but when said low-to-high, it means "a bridge." In western Japan, it's the opposite: High-to-low pitch means "a bridge," and low-to-high pitch means "chopsticks."

How can you tell what anyone means? For one thing, the eastern dialect is standard because that's where Tokyo, Japan's capital, is located. In any event, the context usually makes the meaning clear. If you're in a restaurant and you ask for **hashi,** you can safely assume that, no matter how you pitch this word, no one will bring you a bridge.

Here's another interesting fact about pitch: The Japanese raise their overall pitch when speaking to their superiors. This pitch change is most noticeable among women. Female workers raise their pitch quite a bit when dealing with customers. Women also raise their pitch when speaking to young children.

You Already Know a Little Japanese

Believe it or not, you already know many Japanese words: Some are Japanese words that English borrowed and incorporated, and others are English words used in Japan.

Japanese words in English

Do you love **sushi**? Do you practice **karate**? Do you hang out at **karaoke** bars? Even if you answered no to every question, you probably know what these words mean and know that they come from Japanese.

Check out these other words that traveled from Japan to become part of the English language:

- ✔ **hibachi** (hee-bah-chee; a portable charcoal stove)
- ✔ **jūdō** (jooo-dohh; a Japanese martial art that redirects an attack back onto the attacker)
- ✔ **kimono** (kee-moh-noh; a robe with wide sleeves and a sash; traditional Japanese clothing for women)
- ✔ **origami** (oh-ree-gah-mee; the art of paper folding)
- ✔ **sake** (sah-keh; Japanese rice wine)
- ✔ **samurai** (sah-moo-rah-ee; professional warriors)
- ✔ **sashimi** (sah-shee-mee; sliced raw fish)
- ✔ **sukiyaki** (soo-kee-yah-kee; Japanese-style beef stew)
- ✔ **tsunami** (tsoo-nah-mee; tidal wave)

English words used in Japanese

Many English words have crossed the ocean to Japan, and that number is increasing quickly. You can use many English words in Japan — if you pronounce them with a heavy Japanese accent:

- ✔ **jūsu** (jooo-soo; juice)
- ✔ **kamera** (kah-meh-rah; camera)
- ✔ **kōhī** (kohh-heee; coffee)
- ✔ **nekutai** (neh-koo-tah-ee; necktie)
- ✔ **pātī** (pahh-teee; party)

Puzzling English words in Japan

Some English words changed their meanings after being assimilated into the Japanese language. Don't be puzzled when you hear these words:

✔ Smart: **Sumāto** (soo-mahh-toh) doesn't mean bright. It means "skinny" or "thin" in Japan.

✔ Training pants: **Torēningu pantsu** (toh-rehh-neen-goo pahn-tsoo) aren't for toddlers who are about to give up their diapers. They're gym pants, and adults wear them, too.

✔ Mansion: **Manshon** (mahn-shohn) isn't a huge, gorgeous house. It's just a small, neat-looking condominium in Japan.

✔ **rajio** (rah-jee-oh; radio)

✔ **resutoran** (reh-soo-toh-rahn; restaurant)

✔ **sutēki** (soo-tehh-kee; steak)

✔ **sutoraiku** (soo-toh-rah-ee-koo; strike)

Picking Up Some Basic Phrases

Start using the following short Japanese phrases at home. You may need your family's cooperation, but if you make it a habit, you'll be amazed at how quickly you pick up a bit of Japanese.

✔ **Dōmo** (dohh-moh; Thank you *or* Hi!)

✔ **Īe** (eee-eh; No *or* Don't mention it.)

✔ **Hai** (hah-ee; Yes)

✔ **Wakarimasen** (wah-kah-ree-mah-sen; I don't understand.)

- **Shirimasen** (she-ree-mah-sen; I don't know the answer to that question.)

- **Sō, sō** (sohh, sohh; You're right, you're right!)

  Used when you agree with someone's statement. This phrase is similar to what you mean when you say "yeah" in the middle of an English conversation just to let the other person know that you're listening.

- **Dame** (dah-meh; You're not allowed to do that *or* That's bad!)

  Used when you want to stop someone from doing something or when you want to say that something is bad or impermissible. You'd never say this phrase to a superior or to someone older than you. You can say it to children, siblings, or very close friends.

- **Zenzen** (zehn-zehn; Not at all *or* It was nothing.)

- **Ii desu ne** (ee-ee deh-soo neh; That's a great idea!)

- **Yatta** (yaht-tah; Yahoo! I did it.)

- **Gambatte** (gahm-baht-teh; Go for it! *or* Try your best!)

- **Omedetō** (oh-meh-deh-tohh; Congratulations!)

- **Yōkoso** (yohh-koh-soh; Welcome!)

- **Shinpai shinaide** (sheen-pah-ee shee-nah-ee-deh; Don't worry!)

- **Makasete** (mah-kah-seh-teh; Count on me!)

Chapter 2

Grammar on a Diet: Just the Basics

*I*f grammar rules are the branches of a tree, then words are the tree's foliage. Checking the branches before enjoying those leaves is the shortcut to your success in understanding the entire tree. In this chapter, I show you what the branches of the Japanese language tree look like.

Using Appropriate Speech Styles

The Japanese use different speech styles depending on who they're talking to. For example, you ask a simple question like "Did you see it?" differently of different people:

> ✔ When speaking to a superior, like your boss, use the *formal* style of speech and say **Goran ni narimashita ka** (goh-rahn nee nah-ree-mah-shee-tah kah).

- When speaking to a colleague, use the *polite/neutral* style and say **Mimashita ka** (mee-mah-shee-tah kah).

- With kids, use the *plain/informal* style and say **Mita no** (mee-tah noh).

Notice that the phrase becomes shorter and shorter as you go down the hierarchy.

The tricky part is that the correct speech style depends on both social hierarchy, in terms of position and age, and social grouping, such as insiders and outsiders (see Chapter 10). The informal form can sound rude, but also very friendly; the formal form can sound very polite, but also awfully cold. And what if your assistant is older than you? What if your son is also your boss? In some cases, which style you should use is unclear. Table 2-1 gives you some general guidelines.

Table 2-1	Speech Styles
Style	*Whom to Use It With*
Formal	A customer, a person who's much older than you, your boss, your teacher
Polite/neutral	A classmate, a colleague, a neighbor, an acquaintance, a friend's parent
Plain/informal	Your parent, your child, your spouse, your student, your assistant, a close friend

When in doubt, use the polite/neutral style.

Forming Sentences

The basic word order in English is subject-verb-object. In Japanese, it's subject-object-verb. Instead of saying "I watched TV," for example, you say "I TV watched." Instead of saying "I ate sushi," you say "I sushi ate." Repeat after me: Put the *verb at the end! Verb end!*

Introducing particles

Subject-object-verb is the basic word order in Japanese, but object-subject-verb is also okay. As long as the verb is at the end of the sentence, Japanese grammar teachers are happy. For example, if Mary invited John, you can say either "Mary John invited" or "John Mary invited" in Japanese.

A smart person like you may say, "Wait a minute! How do you know who invited whom?" The secret is that Japanese uses a tag called a *particle* after each noun phrase. The particle for the action performer (the subject) is **ga** (gah), and the particle for the action receiver (the direct object) is **o** (oh). So both the following sentences mean "Mary invited John":

- ✔ **Marī ga Jon o sasotta.** (mah-reee gah john oh sah-soht-tah)
- ✔ **Jon o Marī ga sasotta.** (john oh mah-reee gah sah-soht-tah)

Other Japanese particles include **kara** (kah-rah), **made** (mah-deh), **ni** (nee), **de** (deh), **to** (toh), and **ka** (kah). Luckily, they can be translated into English words like *from, until, to, with, by, at, in, on, and,* and *or.* But each particle is translated differently depending on the context. For example, the particle **de** corresponds to *in, by,* or *with* in English:

- ✔ **Bosuton de benkyō suru.** (boh-soo-tohn deh behn-kyohh soo-roo; I'll study in Boston.)
- ✔ **Takushī de iku.** (tah-koo-sheee deh ee-koo; I'll go by taxi.)
- ✔ **Fōku de taberu.** (fohh-koo deh tah-beh-roo; I eat with a fork.)

Remember the particles in terms of their general functions, not their English translations. Table 2-2 presents the Japanese particles and their various meanings.

Table 2-2 Particles

Particle	Translation	General Function	Example
ga (gah)	No English equivalent	Specifies the subject of the sentence	Jon ga kita. (john gah kee-tah; John came.)
o (oh)	No English equivalent	Specifies the direct object of the sentence	Marī ga Jon o sasotta. (mah-reee gah john oh sah-soht-tah; Mary invited John.)
kara (kah-rah)	from	Specifies the starting point of the action	Ku-ji kara benkyō shita. (koo-jee kah-rah behn-kyohh shee-tah; I studied from 9:00.)
made (mah-deh)	until	Specifies the ending point of the action	San-ji made benkyō shita. (sahn-jee mah-deh behn-kyohh shee-tah; I studied until 3:00.)
ni (nee)	to, on, at	Specifies the target of the action	Nihon ni itta. (nee-hohn nee eet-tah; I went to Japan.) Tōkyō ni tsuita. (tohh-kyohh nee tsoo-ee-tah; I arrived at Tokyo.)
ni (nee)	to, on, at	Specifies the time of the event	San-ji ni tsuita. (sahn-jee nee tsoo-ee-tah; I arrived at 3:00.)

Particle	Translation	General Function	Example
e (eh)	to, toward	Specifies the direction of the action	Tōkyō e itta. (tohh-kyohh eh eet-tah; I went to Tokyo.)
de (deh)	in, by, with, at	Specifies how the action takes place; indicates the location, manner, or background condition of the action	Bosuton de benkyō shita. (boh-soo-tohn de behn-kyohh shee-tah; I studied in Boston.) Takushī de itta. (tah-koo sheee deh eet-tah; I went there by taxi.) Fōku de tabeta. (fohh-koo deh tah-beh-tah; I ate with a fork.)
no (noh)	's	Creates a possessive phrase or modifier phrase	Marī no hon (mah-reee noh hohn; Mary's book) Nihongo no hon (nee-hon-goh noh hohn; A Japanese language book)
to (toh)	and	Lists items	Sushi to sashimi o tabeta. (soo-shee toh sah-shee-mee oh tah-beh-tah; I ate sushi and sashimi.)
to (toh)	with	Specifies an item with the same status as the subject	Jon ga Marī to utatta. (john gah mah-reee toh oo-taht-tah; John sang with Mary.)
ka (kah)	or	Lists choices	Sushi ka sashimi o taberu. (soo-shee kah sah-shee-mee oh tah-beh-roo; I will eat sushi or sashimi.)

You can have a bunch of particles in a sentence, as in these examples:

- ✔ **Marī ga kuruma de Tōkyō e itta.** (mah-reee gah koo-roo-mah deh tohh-kyohh eh eet-tah; Mary went to Tokyo by car.)

- ✔ **Jon no otōsan kara bīru to osake to wain o moratta.** (john noh oh-tohh-sahn kah-rah beee-roo toh oh-sah-keh toh wah-een oh moh-raht-tah; I received beer, sake, and wine from John's dad.)

> Japanese nouns need these particles, but they don't need articles like *a* and *the* in English. Furthermore, you don't need to specify singular or plural. **Tamago** (tah-mah-goh) means either "an egg" or "eggs."

Telling the topic

The Japanese love mentioning topics at the beginning of their sentences. If you put a topic phrase at the beginning of whatever you say, you'll sound a lot more like a native Japanese speaker.

At the beginning of a statement, clarify what you're talking about by providing the listener with a heads-up: "As for **topic**" or "Speaking of **topic**." Use the particle **wa** (wah) to mark the topic word. Suppose you're talking about what you did yesterday. Start with the word for yesterday, **kino** (kee-nohh), add **wa** after **kino** to alert the listener that yesterday is your topic, and then finish the sentence.

The following sentences differ in what the speaker is talking about. The statement can be about what happened *yesterday,* what happened to *the teacher,* or what happened to *John,* depending on what precedes **wa:**

- ✔ **Kinō wa sensei ga Jon o shikatta.** (kee-nohh wah sehn-sehh gah john oh shee-kaht-tah; As for yesterday, what happened is that the teacher scolded John.)

✔ **Sensei wa kinō Jon o shikatta.** (sehn-sehh wah kee-nohh john oh shee-kaht-tah; As for the teacher, what he did yesterday was to scold John.)

✔ **Jon wa sensei ga kinō shikatta.** (john wah sehn-sehh gah kee-nohh shee-kaht-tah; As for John, what happened was that the teacher scolded him yesterday.)

When a noun is both the subject and the topic of a sentence, you use only the topic particle **wa** — never **ga wa** — to mark the noun. When a noun is the direct object as well as the topic, you mark it with **wa** — never with both **o** and **wa**.

Dropping Understood Words

The Japanese use the minimum number of words necessary to convey their meaning. Minimalist speaking is the Japanese way.

One way you can pare down sentences is to drop pronouns and words that are understood in context. The Japanese drop both almost all the time. As a result, you often hear sentences without a subject, direct object, time phrase, or location phrase. Seeing a sentence that consists of just the verb or the topic isn't uncommon. For example, you don't have to speak the underlined words in the following sentences:

✔ **Hotto doggu wa <u>tabemasu ka</u>.** [hoht-toh dohg-goo wah (tah-beh-mah-soo kah); Will you eat a hot dog?]

✔ **<u>Watashi wa kinō</u> tenisu o <u>shimashita</u>.** [(wah-tah-shee wah kee-nohh teh-nee-soo oh) shee-mah-shee-tah; I played tennis yesterday.]

Using Pronouns

Pronouns are convenient shorthand for nouns that both English and Japanese make good use of. Check out the following instruction, where all the pronouns are italicized:

Mix *those* together like *this,* leave *it* right *there* for a while, and then give *it* to *him* with *that.*

Demonstrative pronouns

Demonstrative pronouns seems like much too big a term to describe four little words: *this, that, these,* and *those.* You use demonstrative pronouns to "point" verbally.

In Japanese, demonstrative pronouns are just a little more complicated than they are in English. Suppose you're the speaker and your girlfriend is the listener, and the two of you are sitting face to face at a cozy table in a restaurant. In this case, the half of the table on your side is your territory, and the half on your girlfriend's side is her territory. All other tables in the restaurant are outside both your territories. With these boundaries drawn, you can use the following pronouns when referring to various foods throughout the restaurant:

- ✔ **kore** (koh-reh): Things in your territory
- ✔ **sore** (soh-reh): Things in her territory
- ✔ **are** (ah-reh): Things outside both your territories

Do you get the idea? If you do, you can understand who's eating **tako** (tah-koh; octopus), who's eating **ika** (ee-kah; squid), and who's eating **ebi** (eh-bee; shrimp) at the restaurant in the following dialogue:

Sore wa ika desu ka. (soh-reh wah ee-kah deh-soo kah; Is that squid?)

Ie, kore wa tako desu. Sore wa ika desu ka. (eee-eh, koh-ree wah tah-koh deh-soo. soh-ree wah ee-kah deh-soo kah; No, this one is octopus. Is that one squid?)

Hai, kore wa ika desu. (hah-ee, koh-reh wah ee-kah deh-soo; Yes, this one is squid.)

Jā, are wa nan desu ka. (jahh, ah-reh wah nahn deh-soo kah; Then what is that one over there?)

Are wa ebi desu. (ah-reh wah eh-bee deh-soo; That one over there is shrimp.)

Personal pronouns

The first-person singular pronoun in Japanese is **watashi** (wah-tah-shee), which corresponds to the English *I* and *me*. Japanese does have other personal pronouns, which you can find in Table 2-3.

Table 2-3	Personal Pronouns	
Pronoun	*Pronunciation*	*Translation*
watashi	wah-tah-shee	I, me
watashitachi	wah-tah-shee-tah-chee	we, us
anata	ah-nah-tah	you (singular)
anatatachi	ah-nah-tah-tah-chee	you (plural)
kare	kah-reh	he, him
karera	kah-reh-ah	they, them (male and mixed genders)
kanojo	kah-noh-joh	she, her
kanojora	kah-noh-joh-rah	they, them (female)

The first-person singular pronoun is typically **watashi,** but you can say *I/me* in more than one way:

✔ The formal version is **watakushi** (wah-tah-koo-shee).

✔ In informal and neutral contexts, men say **boku** (boh-koo).

✔ In informal contexts, some men say **ore** (oh-reh), some older men say **washi** (wah-shee), and some young women say **atashi** (ah-tah-shee).

The first-person pronouns are used repeatedly in conversation, but other pronouns aren't. In fact, the use of **anata** (ah-nah-tah; you, singular) is almost forbidden. A person who says **anata** sounds snobbish, arrogant, or just foreign.

So how can you ask a question like **Anata wa ikimasu ka** (ah-nah-tah wa ee-kee-mah-soo kah, Will you go there?) without using **anata**? One strategy is to drop the pronoun. Just use the verb and the question particle: **Ikimasu ka** [ee-kee-mah-soo kah; Will (you) go (there)?]. Another strategy is to use the person's name repeatedly. You can ask Yōko this question: **Yōko-san, Yōko-san wa ikimasu ka** (yohh-koh-sahn, yohh-koh-sahn wah ee-kee-mah-soo kah; literally, Yoko, is Yoko going?), which actually means "Yoko, are you going there?"

Words to Know

are	ah-reh	that one (over there)
kore	koh-reh	this one
sore	soh-reh	that one (near you)
watashi	wah-tah-shee	I/me
boku	boh-koo	I/me (for men)

Working with Verbs

Good news! You don't need to conjugate verbs based on person, gender, or number in Japanese. You use the same form of a verb whether you're talking about yourself, your girlfriend, your boyfriend, or all your friends. For example, you use the verb **taberu** (tah-beh-roo) whether you want to say "I eat," "you eat," "he eats," "she eats," or "they eat."

I'm not saying that Japanese verbs aren't conjugated at all — they are. This section walks you through the various conjugations, showing you how to create present, past, negative, and polite verbs (for more on polite verbs, see the section "Speaking politely").

Japanese places a lot of emphasis on verbs. Verbs not only express actions or states of being, but they also indicate social status, respect, and humility. You can often tell whether a Japanese speaker is talking to an esteemed guest, a colleague, a spouse, or even a dog just by the verb he uses. Throughout this book, I use examples of formal verbs, polite/neutral verbs, and plain/informal verbs. However, the most commonly used verbs fall into the plain/informal and polite/neutral categories.

Understanding basic verb forms

The variations of any Japanese verb are made from four basic verb forms: dictionary form, negative form, stem form, and te-form. By adding things to the ends of these verb forms, replacing the ending sounds with another sound, or, in some cases, using them the way they are, Japanese expresses tense and level of formality, and prepares the verb to accept a *helping verb* (like *is* or *has been* in English). Here are explanations of the four forms:

> ✔ **Dictionary form:** You see this verb form when you look up words in the dictionary. It's kind of like an infinitive in English, but without the *to*.

It's also called the *informal* or *plain form* because you use it when speaking informally to friends or family.

✓ **Negative form:** The opposite of the dictionary form. If the dictionary form means "I do," the negative form means "I don't."

✓ **Stem form:** This is the shortest form of a verb, but it can't stand alone — it needs a verb suffix that indicates tense or some other condition. For example, you add **masu** (mah-soo) to this form to make an affirmative polite verb.

✓ **Te-form:** Called the te-form because most end in **te** (teh) or **de** (deh). This form is commonly used in combination with other verbs or with other helping verbs. By itself, it's understood as an informal request.

When I introduce a new verb, I give you the four forms in this order — dictionary, negative, stem, and te-form — along with the pronunciation. The following is an example with **taberu** (tah-beh-roo; to eat).

Form	Pronunciation
taberu	tah-beh-roo
tabenai	tah-beh-nah-ee
tabe	tah-beh
tabete	tah-beh-teh

Doing the conjugation thing

Like English, Japanese has regular and irregular verbs. All *regular verbs* conjugate according to a predictable pattern, while *irregular verbs* deviate from the pattern. Luckily, most verbs are regular.

Regular verbs come in two basic varieties: *ru-verbs* and *u-verbs.* Before you can conjugate any regular verb, you have to determine which type you're dealing with. Although all ru-verbs end in **ru,** some u-verbs do, too. Unfortunately, a verb's ending tells whether it's a ru-verb or a u-verb only about 80 percent of the time.

To find out whether a word ending in **ru** is a ru-verb or a u-verb, you have to try to conjugate it. If the conjugated form still has that final *r* in it, then the verb is a u-verb. If the conjugated form no longer has an r in it, then the verb is a ru-verb. The word **kaeru** is a good example because it comes in both forms and has two meanings. Look at the following chart. Notice how the ru-verb **kaeru** drops the *r* when it's conjugated, but the u-verb form doesn't.

Form	Ru-verb (To Exchange)	U-verb (To Go Home)
Dictionary	kaeru	kaeru
Negative	kaenai	kaeranai
Stem	kae	kaeri
Te	kaete	kaette

Table 2-4 lists the conjugations of some frequently used ru-verbs.

Table 2-4		Ru-verbs		
Dictionary Form	**Negative Form**	**Stem Form**	**Te-form**	**Meaning**
taberu	tabenai	tabe	tabete	to eat
miru	minai	mi	mite	to watch
iru	inai	i	ite	to exist (people & animals)

Table 2-5 lists the conjugations of some frequently used u-verbs.

Table 2-5		U-verbs		
Dictionary Form	*Negative Form*	*Stem Form*	*Te-form*	*Meaning*
hanasu	hanasanai	hanashi	hanashite	to speak
kaku	kakanai	kaki	kaite	to write
oyogu	oyoganai	oyogi	oyoide	to swim
nomu	nomanai	nomi	nonde	to drink
asobu	asobanai	asobi	asonde	to play
shinu	shinanai	shini	shinde	to die
kau	kawanai	kai	katte	to buy
toru	toranai	tori	totte	to take
matsu	matanai	machi	matte	to wait

Table 2-6 lists the conjugations of some frequently used irregular verbs.

Table 2-6		Irregular Verbs		
Dictionary Form	*Negative Form*	*Stem Form*	*Te-form*	*Meaning*
aru	nai	ari	atte	to exist (inanimate things)
iku	ikanai	iki	itte	to go
kuru	konai	ki	kite	to come
irassharu	irassharanai	irasshai	irasshatte	to exist, come, go (honorific)
suru	shinai	shi	shite	to do

Don't worry too much about conjugating verbs accurately. Pay more attention to how verbs are used in context. When you get a grasp of the functions and implications of each verb form in context, you can start working on remembering detailed rules for producing the correct form.

If you want to try conjugating, pay attention to the ending syllable and the type of verb and follow the pattern of one of the verbs in the preceding tables. But which pattern? Pick the one with the same ending syllable and the same verb type. By *ending syllable,* I mean the last *syllable,* not the last *sound* — that is, the last consonant-vowel combination. If the word doesn't have a consonant before the last vowel, the last vowel itself is the ending syllable of the verb. All the verbs in the dictionary form in the preceding table (and every other verb) end in one of these syllables: **ru, su, ku, gu, mu, bu, nu, u,** and **tsu.** By *verb type,* I mean the u-verb, ru-verb, or irregular verb distinction. Because you can't always tell a verb's type from its ending, I let you know the verb's type whenever I give you a conjugation.

Deciding on tense: Past or not past, that is the question

Japanese verbs have just two tenses: present and past. The dictionary form is present tense. Present tense refers to both present and future, which makes the verb **taberu** not just "I eat," but also "I will eat." The context usually tells you which meaning the verb is expressing. As in English, the present tense often doesn't refer to this very moment but to some habitual action, such as "I eat dinner every day at 6:00."

If you know a verb's te-form, expressing that verb in the past tense is easy. You simply change the final vowel from an **e** to an **a.** For example, **tabete** (tah-beh-teh; eat) becomes **tabeta** (tah-beh-tah; ate), and **nonde** (nohn-deh; drink) becomes **nonda** (nohn-dah; drank).

To say that you didn't do something in the past, you need to fashion verbs into their negative past forms. Simply take the negative form, drop the final vowel, **i,** and add **-katta.** For example, **tabenai** (tah-beh-nah-ee; don't eat) becomes **tabenakatta** (tah-beh-nah-kaht-tah; didn't eat). Cool, huh?

Speaking politely

In Japanese, the verbs you choose say a lot about you. Although using the plain/informal verb form when you talk with close friends or family members is fine, if you use them in a business situation or with strangers, the listener may think you're unsophisticated or even rude. Judging the situation and knowing what level of formality is appropriate is an integral part of speaking Japanese.

Making polite/neutral verb forms is easy. You just have to remember four verb endings (one each for the affirmative present, negative present, affirmative past, and negative past) and add one of them to the end of the verb's stem form.

- ✔ For affirmative present verbs, add **-masu.**
- ✔ For negative present verbs, add **-masen.**
- ✔ For affirmative past verbs, add **-mashita.**
- ✔ For negative past verbs, add **-masen deshita.**

Table 2-7 gives you some examples.

Table 2-7	Making Polite/Neutral Verb Forms		
	taberu [ru] (eat)	*miru [ru] (watch)*	*nomu [u] (drink)*
Stem	tabe	mi	nomi
Affirmative Present	tabemasu	mimasu	nomimasu
Negative Present	tabemasen	mimasen	nomimasen

	taberu [ru] (eat)	*miru [ru] (watch)*	*nomu [u] (drink)*
Affirmative Past	tabemashita	mimashita	nomimashita
Negative Past	tabemasen deshita	mimasen deshita	nomimasen deshita

Enhancing verbs with suffixes

Japanese has a rich inventory of verb suffixes that add either concrete meaning or subtle implications. Different suffixes require different verb forms: *plain/informal form* (dictionary form, negative form, past tense, or negative past tense), stem form, or te-form. You may think that I'm slipping a whole new form in on you, but *plain/informal form* is just the term I use to indicate that the verb form *isn't* the stem or the te-form. Dictionary form, negative form, past tense, and negative past tense verbs all follow the same pattern, so I call them all the plain/informal form. Table 2-8 shows some of the most common suffixes.

Note: In this table, I use hyphens to show you the boundary between the verb and the verb suffix, but you pronounce the verbs as one word or phrase.

Table 2-8	Common Verb Suffixes		
Meaning/ Function	*Suffix*	*Example*	*Translation*
Suffixes that Follow Plain/Informal Forms			
should	-beki desu	taberu-beki desu	I should eat.
probability	-deshō	taberu-deshō	I'll probably eat.
possibility	-kamo shiremasen	taberu-kamo shiremasen	I might eat.

(continued)

Table 2-8 *(continued)*

Meaning/ Function	Suffix	Example	Translation
person	-hito	taberu-hito	the person who eats
because	-kara	taberu-kara	because I eat
noun-maker	-koto	taberu-koto	the act of eating
things	-mono	taberu-mono	things to eat
time	-toki	taberu-toki	when I eat
intention	-tsumori desu	taberu-tsumori desu	I plan to eat.
Suffixes that Follow Stem Forms			
while	-nagara	tabe-nagara	while eating
purpose	-ni	tabe-ni	in order to eat
difficulty	-nikui	tabe-nikui	It's hard to eat.
overdoing	-sugiru	tabe-sugiru	I overeat.
desire	-tai	tabe-tai	I want to eat.
Suffixes that Follow Te-forms			
doing a favor	-ageru	tabete-ageru	I eat for you.
present perfect	-aru	tabete-aru	I have eaten.
present progressive	-iru	tabete-iru	I am eating.
requesting	-kudasai	tabete-kudasai	Please eat.
attempt	-miru	tabete-miru	I'll try to eat.
completion	-shimau	tabete-shimau	I finish eating.

Using the Verb Desu (To Be)

Like the English verb *to be,* **desu** (deh-soo) expresses
the identity or state of people and things. **Desu** is
used in a construction, **X wa Y desu** (X wah Y deh-
soo; X is Y). Instead of saying "X is Y," the Japanese
say "X Y is." The particle **wa** (wah) is the topic particle discussed earlier in this chapter.

Desu follows either a noun or an adjective. For example, **Otōto wa gakusē desu** (oh-tohh-toh wah gah-koo-
sehh deh-soo) means "My little brother is a student."
Watashi wa genki desu (wah-tah-shee wah gehn-kee
deh-soo) means "I am fine." Now you know why many
Japanese sentences end in **desu.**

Conjugation-wise, **desu** doesn't look like any other
verb. The reason is that **desu** didn't start out as a
stand-alone verb. It was the combination of the particle **de,** the verb **aru** (ah-roo; to exist), and the polite
suffix -**masu.**

Table 2-9 shows the patterns of **desu.** To help you see
the point, I use the same noun **gakusē** (gah-koo-sehh;
student) in each example.

Table 2-9	Formal Form of Noun Plus Desu	
Japanese	*Pronunciation*	*Translation*
gakusei desu	gah-koo-sehh deh-soo	is a student
gakusei ja arimasen	gah-koo-sehh jah ah-ree-mah-sehn	isn't a student
gakusei deshita	gah-koo-sehh deh-shee-tah	was a student
gakusei ja arimasen deshita	gah-koo-sehh jah ah-ree-mah-sehn deh-shee-tah	wasn't a student

In an informal context, you use the shorter version of **desu,** as Table 2-10 demonstrates.

Table 2-10	Informal Form of Noun Plus Desu	
Japanese	*Pronunciation*	*Translation*
gakusei da	gah-koo-sehh dah	is a student
gakusei ja nai	gah-koo-sehh jah nah-ee	isn't a student
gakusei datta	gah-koo-sehh daht-tah	was a student
gakusei ja nakatta	gah-koo-sehh jah nah-kaht-tah	wasn't a student

Ja (jah), which you see in the negative forms in Tables 2-9 and 2-10, is the contraction of **dewa** (deh-wah). Most Japanese people use **ja** in everyday conversation, but they use **dewa** occasionally. Be prepared to hear either one.

Describing Adjectives

As in English, Japanese adjectives are placed either before a noun (a *good* book, for example) or at the end of a sentence (The book is *good*).

All Japanese adjectives end in either *i* or *na* when placed before a noun. Adjectives that end in *i* are called *i-type adjectives,* and adjectives that end in *na* are called *na-type adjectives.* There's really no clear-cut distinction between the two groups in terms of meaning. For example, **taka-i** and **kōka-na** both mean "expensive," but one is an i-type adjective and the other is a na-type adjective.

Look at some adjectives that modify the noun **hon** (hohn; book):

✔ **kirei-na hon** (kee-rehh-nah hohn; a beautiful book)

✔ **kōka-na hon** (kohh-kah-nah hohn; an expensive book)

✔ **omoshiro-i hon** (oh-moh-shee-roh-ee hohn; an interesting book)

✔ **taka-i hon** (tah-kah-ee hohn; an expensive book)

You conjugate English adjectives based on whether they're comparative or superlative, like *tall, taller,* and *tallest,* but you conjugate Japanese adjectives based on different factors, such as tense (see the chart below for examples). When you place adjectives at the end of a sentence rather than before a noun, the *i* and *na* change or disappear, and an extra item like the verb **desu** (deh-soo; to be) shows up. The form of **desu** depends on the tense, whether it's affirmative or negative, and whether it's plain/informal or polite/neutral.

Look at the following sentences, all of which include either **taka-i** (tah-kah-ee; expensive), an i-type adjective, or **kōka-na** (kohh-kah-nah; expensive), a na-type adjective:

✔ **Are wa kōka ja arimasen.** (ah-reh wah kohh-kah jah ah-ree-mah-sehn; That is not expensive.)

✔ **Hanbāgā wa taka-ku arimasen.** (hahn-bahh-gahh wah tah-kah-koo ah-ree-mah-sehn; Hamburgers are not expensive.)

✔ **Kōka-na nekkuresu o kaimashita.** (kohh-kah nah nehk-koo-reh-soo oh kah-ee-mah-shee-tah; I bought an expensive necklace.)

✔ **Kore wa taka-katta.** (koh-reh wah tah-kah-kaht-tah; This was expensive.)

✔ **Taka-i hon o kaimashita.** (tah-kah-ee hohn oh kah-ee-mah-shee-tah; I bought an expensive book.)

Table 2-11 summarizes the patterns for i-type and na-type adjectives, along with variations in parentheses.

Table 2-11	Adjective Patterns	
Tense/ Polarity	*I-type*	*Na-type*
Plain/Informal Style		
Present affirmative (is)	taka-i	kōka na
Present negative (isn't)	taka-ku nai	kōka ja nai
Past affirmative (was)	taka-katta	kōka datta
Past negative (wasn't)	taka-ku nakatta	kōka ja nakatta
Polite/Neutral Style		
Present affirmative (is)	taka-i desu	kōka desu
Present negative (isn't)	taka-ku arimasen (taka-ku nai desu)	kōka ja arimasen (kōka ja nai desu)
Past affirmative (was)	taka-katta desu	kōka deshita
Past negative (wasn't)	taka-ku arimasen deshita (taka-ku nakatta desu)	kōka ja arimasen deshita (kōka ja nakatta desu)

Some adjectives are irregular, which means they don't conjugate the same as other adjectives. The irregular adjective used most frequently is **i-i** (ee-ee; good). The stem **i** becomes **yo** in all the forms except the present affirmative form, regardless of whether you place it at the end of a sentence or right before a noun. Take a look at the following examples:

- ✔ **i-i hon desu** (ee-ee hohn deh-soo; is a good book)
- ✔ **i-i-desu** (ee-ee deh-soo; is good)
- ✔ **yo-katta desu** (yoh-kaht-tah deh-soo; was good)
- ✔ **yo-ku arimasen deshita** (yoh-koo ah-ree-mah-sehn deh-shee-tah; wasn't good)
- ✔ **yo-ku arimasen** (yoh-koo ah-ree-mah-sen; isn't good)

Chapter 3

Numerical Gumbo: Counting of All Kinds

. . . .

In This Chapter

▶ Working with numbers

▶ Counting years, months, weeks, and days

▶ Knowing the time

▶ Visiting a bank

. . . .

*N*umbers are an indispensable part of life. When you cook, you count the number of eggs you put into your batter. When you're at a party, your spouse counts the number of drinks you have. When you get paid, you count the number of bills in your hand. Well, now you can count those bills in Japanese.

Knowing Your Numbers

Numbers are a great place to start discovering Japanese. Start at 1 and work your way up!

Numbers from 1 to 10

You can master the art of counting from 1 to 10 right now. Check out Table 3-1.

Table 3-1	Numbers from 1 to 10	
Number	**Japanese**	**Pronunciation**
1	ichi	ee-chee
2	ni	nee
3	san	sahn
4	yon; shi	yohn; shee
5	go	goh
6	roku	roh-koo
7	nana; shichi	nah-nah; shee-chee
8	hachi	hah-chee
9	kyū; ku	kyooo; koo
10	jū	jooo

The numbers that follow a semicolon in Table 3-1 are used for reciting numbers or doing arithmetic — not for counting.

Numbers from 11 to 99

The Japanese number system is both cumbersome and logical. The concept of lucky and unlucky numbers is the cumbersome part. The Japanese think that 3, 5, and 7 are lucky numbers and that 4 and 9 are unlucky. So the next time you give cookies to a Japanese person, give any number except 4 or 9.

And now for the logical part: To make any number from 11 to 99, you combine the numbers 1 to 10. For example:

- ✔ 11 is **jū-ichi** (jooo-ee-chee) — 10 (**jū**) plus 1 (**ichi**).
- ✔ 12 is **jū-ni** (jooo-nee) — 10 (**jū**) plus 2 (**ni**).

✔ 20 is two sets of ten, so you say "two tens," or **ni-jū** (nee-jooo).

✔ 21 is **ni-jū-ichi** (nee-jooo-ee-chee) — 20 (**ni-jū**) plus 1 (**ichi**).

You can use this pattern to count to **kyū-jū-kyū** (kyooo-jooo-kyooo; 99, or 9 tens plus 9).

Numbers from 100 to 9,999

To count over 100, keep using the pattern for numbers 11 to 99:

✔ 100 is **hyaku** (hyah-koo), so 200 is **ni-hyaku** (nee-hyah-koo).

✔ 1,000 is **sen** (sehn), so 2,000 is **ni-sen** (nee-sehn).

Be aware of some irregular sound changes. When the words for 100, **hyaku,** and 1,000, **sen,** are preceded by the number 3, **san,** they become **byaku** (byah-koo) and **zen** (zehn), respectively. So 300 is **san-byaku** and 3,000 is **san-zen.** Other irregular sound changes occur in 600, **rop-pyaku** (rohp-pyah-koo); 800, **hap-pyaku** (hahp-pyah-koo); and 8,000, **has-sen** (hahs-sehn). Table 3-2 lists some of the numbers from 100 to 9,000.

Table 3-2	Select Numbers from 100 to 9,000	
Number	**Japanese**	**Pronunciation**
100	hyaku	hyah-koo
200	ni-hyaku	nee-hyah-koo
300	san-byaku	sahn-byah-koo
400	yon-hyaku	yohn-hyah-koo
500	go-hyaku	goh-hyah-koo

(continued)

Table 3-2 (continued)

Number	Japanese	Pronunciation
600	rop-pyaku	rohp-pyah-koo
700	nana-hyaku	nah-nah-hyah-koo
800	hap-pyaku	hahp-pyah-koo
900	kyū-hyaku	kyooo-hyah-koo
1,000	sen	sehn
2,000	ni-sen	nee-sehn
3,000	san-zen	sahn-zehn
4,000	yon-sen	yohn-sehn
5,000	go-sen	goh-sehn
6,000	roku-sen	roh-koo-sehn
7,000	nana-sen	nah-nah-sehn
8,000	has-sen	hahs-sehn
9,000	kyū-sen	kyooo-sehn

Numbers from 10,000 to 100,000

Unlike English, Japanese has a special digit name for
10,000: **man** (mahn). For 50,000, you may want to say
go-jū-sen because your mathematical logic is that
50,000 is **go-jū** (50) of **sen** (1,000), but the Japanese say
go-man (goh-mahn; 50,000). Ten thousand is **ichi-man**
(ee-chee-mahn; 10,000), 20,000 is **ni-man** (nee-mahn;
20,000), and so on. One-hundred thousand isn't 100
sen (thousand) but 10 **man**, or **jū-man.** Getting used to
it? Check out Table 3-3 to compare digit names.

Table 3-3	**Japanese Digit Names**	
Number	**English**	**Japanese**
10	ten	jū
100	hundred	hyaku
1,000	thousand	sen
10,000	N/A	man
1,000,000	million	N/A
100,000,000	N/A	oku

If you're not sure of your counting abilities just yet, look up the numbers over 10,000 in Table 3-4.

Table 3-4	**Selected Numbers from 10,000 to 100,000**	
Number	**Japanese**	**Pronunciation**
10,000	ichi-man	ee-chee-mahn
20,000	ni-man	nee-mahn
30,000	san-man	sahn-mahn
40,000	yon-man	yohn-mahn
50,000	go-man	goh-mahn
60,000	roku-man	roh-koo-mahn
70,000	nana-man	nah-nah-mahn
80,000	hachi-man	hah-chee-mahn
90,000	kyū-man	kyooo-mahn
100,000	jū-man	jooo-mahn

Counting with Counters

If I say "I drank one sake," you don't know whether I drank one glass or one bottle, although my brain function would differ dramatically depending on the answer. And if I eat two dozen eggs instead of two eggs every day, I won't live as long as I should. Words like *glasses, bottles,* and *dozens* express an amount or quantity. Other unit words include *pieces, sheets,* and *pairs* (as in a *piece* of cake, a *sheet* of paper, and a *pair* of shoes).

Unless you're reciting numbers or doing arithmetic, you need to place a counter right after a number. You use *counters* to specify the time and date, talk about your age, chat about your test score, or count days, cars, students, money, fish, and a ton of other things.

The counter you use depends on the shape, size, and type of the item. If you count mechanical items such as cars, for example, you need the counter **-dai** (dah-ee). Simply add the counter after the number of cars — **ichi-dai, ni-dai, san-dai,** and so on. The tricky part is that an item can have more than one counter. When you're at the fish market trying to buy mackerel, for example, you can use either **-hiki** or **-hon**.

Table 3-5 lists common counters and their uses.

Table 3-5	Counters and Their Uses	
Counter	*Use*	*Examples*
-dai (dah-ee)	mechanical items	cars, typewriters, refrigerators
-hiki (hee-kee)	animals	dogs, frogs, fish, mosquitoes

Counter	Use	Examples
-hon (hohn)	cylindrical items	pens, pencils, bananas, sticks, umbrellas
-mai (mah-ee)	flat items	bed sheets, paper, stamps
-nin (neen)	people	students, children, women
-tsu (tsoo)	various inanimate items/items that don't have a specific counter	furniture, apples, bags, traffic lights

Table 3-6 gives you the numbers from 1 to 10 and shows you how to use various counters.

If you forget which counter to use and you're counting no more than 10 of something, the counters in the **-tsu** column of Table 3-6 work for just about anything.

Counting the months

The Japanese word for *moon* is **tsuki** (tsoo-kee), which also means "month." Japanese doesn't have a separate word for each month — it uses a number paired with the counter **-gatsu** (gah-tsoo). For example, January is **ichi-gatsu** (eeh-chee-gah-tsoo).

Table 3-6 **Counting with Counters**

Number	-dai Mechanical Items	-hiki Animals	-hon Cylindrical Items	-mai Flat Items	-nin People	-tsu Various Inanimate Items
1 ichi	ichi-dai	ip-piki	ip-pon	ichi-mai	hitori	hito-tsu
2 ni	ni-dai	ni-hiki	ni-hon	ni-mai	futari	futa-tsu
3 san	san-dai	san-biki	san-bon	san-mai	san-nin	mit-tsu
4 yon	yon-dai	yon-hiki	yon-hon	yon-mai	yo-nin	yot-tsu
5 go	go-dai	go-hiki	go-hon	go-mai	go-nin	itsu-tsu
6 roku	roku-dai	rop-piki	rop-pon	roku-mai	roku-nin	mut-tsu
7 nana	nana-dai	nana-hiki	nana-hon	nana-mai	nana-nin	nana-tsu
8 hachi	hachi-dai	hap-piki	hap-pon	hachi-mai	hachi-nin	yat-tsu
9 kyū	kyū-dai	kyū-hiki	kyū-hon	kyū-mai	kyū-nin	kokono-tsu
10 jū	ju[lil]-dai	jup-piki	jup-pon	jū-mai	jū-nin	tō

Using a number to name a month may seem strange, but English uses numbers to express months, too — April 20 is 4/20, for example. Just add the counter **-gatsu** after the number you normally use to refer to a month — but in Japanese, of course. Table 3-7 lists the 12 **tsuki**.

Table 3-7	The Months	
English	**Japanese**	**Pronunciation**
January	ichi-gatsu	ee-chee-gah-tsoo
February	ni-gatsu	nee-gah-tsoo
March	san-gatsu	sahn-gah-tsoo
April	shi-gatsu	shee-gah-tsoo
May	go-gatsu	goh-gah-tsoo
June	roku-gatsu	roh-koo-gah-tsoo
July	shichi-gatsu	shee-chee-gah-tsoo
August	hachi-gatsu	hah-chee-gah-tsoo
September	ku-gatsu	koo-gah-tsoo
October	jū-gatsu	jooo-gah-tsoo
November	jū-ichi-gatsu	jooo-ee-chee-gah-tsoo
December	jū-ni-gatsu	jooo-nee-gah-tsoo

The number 4 is usually pronounced **yon** (yohn) rather than **shi** (shee) because **shi** is also the word for death.

To express a number of months, use the counter
-kagetsu (kah-geh-tsoo) or **-kagetsukan** (kah-geh-tsoo-
kahn). In conversation, **-kagetsu** is more common, but
it's good to know both. Table 3-8 shows how **kagetsu**
is pronounced when combined with numbers. Watch
out for irregular sound changes!

Table 3-8	Numbers of Months	
English	*Japanese*	*Pronunciation*
1 month	ik-kagetsu	eek-kah-geh-tsoo
2 months	ni-kagetsu	nee-kah-geh-tsoo
3 months	san-kagetsu	sahn-kah-geh-tsoo
4 months	yon-kagetsu	yohn-kah-geh-tsoo
5 months	go-kagetsu	goh-kah-geh-tsoo
6 months	rok-kagetsu	rohk-kah-geh-tsoo
7 months	nana-kagetsu	nah-nah-kah-geh-tsoo
8 months	hachi-kagetsu	hah-chee-kah-geh-tsoo
9 months	kyū-kagetsu	kyooo-kah-geh-tsoo
10 months	juk-kagetsu	jook-kah-geh-tsoo

Counting the days

In this section, I show you how to say "the first," "the
second," and so on for dates and how to specify items
in a sequence, like "the third slice of pizza." To find
out how to say these words in reference to items like
buildings, streets, and intersections, see Chapter 9.

The way dates are pronounced in Japanese is full of
irregularities. Your best bet is to memorize Table 3-9.

Table 3-9		What's Today's Date?
Date	**Japanese**	**Pronunciation**
1st	tsuitachi	tsoo-ee-tah-chee
2nd	futsuka	foo-tsoo-kah
3rd	mikka	meek-kah
4th	yokka	yohk-kah
5th	itsuka	ee-tsoo-kah
6th	muika	moo-ee-kah
7th	nanoka	nah-noh-kah
8th	yōka	yohh-kah
9th	kokonoka	koh-koh-noh-kah
10th	tōka	tohh-kah
11th	11-nichi	jooo-ee-chee-nee-chee
12th	12-nichi	jooo-nee-nee-chee
13th	13-nichi	jooo-sahn-nee-chee
14th	jūyokka	jooo-yohk-kah
15th	15-nichi	jooo-goh-nee-chee
16th	16-nichi	jooo-roh-koo-nee-chee
17th	17-nichi	jooo-shee-chee-nee-chee
18th	18-nichi	jooo-hah-chee-nee-chee
19th	19-nichi	jooo-koo-nee-chee
20th	hatsuka	hah-tsoo-kah
21st	21-nichi	nee-jooo-ee-chee-nee-chee
22nd	22-nichi	nee-jooo-nee-nee-chee
23rd	23-nichi	nee-jooo-sahn-nee-chee

(continued)

Table 3-9 *(continued)*

Date	Japanese	Pronunciation
24th	nijūyokka	nee-jooo-yohk-kah
25th	25-nichi	nee-jooo-goh-nee-chee
26th	26-nichi	nee-jooo-roh-koo-nee-chee
27th	27-nichi	nee-jooo-shee-chee-nee-chee
28th	28-nichi	nee-jooo-hah-chee-nee-chee
29th	29-nichi	nee-jooo-koo-nee-chee
30th	30-nichi	sahn-jooo-nee-chee
31st	31-nichi	sahn-jooo-ee-chee-nee-chee

The dates in Table 3-9 can also be interpreted as the number of days. For example, **11-nichi** can mean either "the 11th" or "11 days." To make it crystal clear that you're talking about the number of days, just add **-kan** (kahn) to this form — **11-nichikan** (jooo-ee-chee-nee-chee-kahn; 11 days). **Tsuitachi,** which means only "the first" and not "one day," is the only exception. To say "one day," say **ichi-nichi** (ee-chee-nee-chee) or **ichi-nichikan** (ee-chee-nee-chee-kahn).

Reeling off the years

The Japanese use two different systems to refer to the year: the Western system and the Japanese system.

To specify the **toshi** (toh-shee; year) using the Western system, add the counter **-nen** after the number that expresses the year — for example, **1998-nen** (sehn-kyooo-hyah-koo-kyooo-jooo-hah-chee-nehn; 1998). Follow this advice and you'll be understood perfectly in Japan.

In the Japanese system, you express years by using the **nengō** (nehn-gohh; era name) and the counter **-nen,** as in **Hēsei 14-nen** (hehh-sehh jooo-yoh-nehn; 2002). A new **nengō** is created every time a new Japanese emperor ascends the throne and continues until another emperor takes his place.

If you want to count years, use either **-nenkan** or **-nen** as counters. So "one year" is **ichi-nen** (ee-chee-nehn) or **ichi-nenkan** (ee-chee-nehn-kahn), and "two years" is **ni-nen** (nee-nehn) or **ni-nenkan** (nee-nehn-kahn). In conversation, the shorter version, **-nen,** is used more frequently than **-nenkan,** but again, it's good to be aware of both forms.

Specifying dates and times

To specify a date in Japanese, start from the largest unit of time, the **toshi** (toh-shee; year), and move to successively smaller units, the **tsuki** (tsoo-kee; month), the **hi** (hee; day of the month), and the **yōbi** (yohh-bee; day of the week) in that order, as in **2002-nen 8-gatsu 29-nichi, mokuyōbi** (nee-sehn-nee-nehn hah-chee-gah-tsoo nee-jooo-koo-nee-chee moh-koo-yohh-bee; August 29, 2002, Thursday).

To specify when something happens or happened, insert a time phrase into the sentence. You can place the time phrase anywhere in the sentence as long as it's before the verb. If you're dealing with a *specific* time — a specific day, month, year, or hour — like **getsuyōbi** (geh-tsoo-yohh-bee; Monday), **shi-gatsu** (shee-gah-tsoo; April), or **7-ji** (shee-chee-jee; 7:00), place the particle **ni** (nee) after the time phrase.

If you're dealing with relative time expressions like **kyonen** (kyoh-nehn; last year), **kyō** (kyohh; today), or **raishū** (rah-ee-shooo; next week), you don't need to use the particle **ni.** Check out the following examples:

✔ **12-gatsu 28-nichi ni ikimasu.** (jooo-nee-gah-tsoo nee-jooo-hah-chee-nee-chee nee ee-kee-mah-soo; I'll go there on December 28.)

✔ **1989-nen ni Hawai ni ikimashita.** (sehn-kyooo-hyah-koo-hah-chee-jooo-kyooo-nehn nee hah-wah-ee nee ee-kee-mah-shee-tah; I went to Hawaii in 1989.)

✔ **Nan-gatsu ni umaremashita ka.** (nahn-gah-tsoo nee oo-mah-reh-mah-shee-tah kah; Which month were you born in?)

✔ **Kyō ēga o mimasu.** (kyohh ehh-gah oh mee-mah-soo; I'll see a movie today.)

✔ **Senshū o-kane o haraimashita.** (sehn-shooo oh-kah-neh oh hah-rah-ee-mah-shee-tah; I paid last week.)

To list a number of activities in the same sentence, put all the verbs except the last one in the te-form. You don't need to use a particle that would correspond to *and* in English — converting all the verbs except the last one into the te-form handles the *and* concept. The last verb expresses the tense of all the activities, as in these examples:

✔ **Kinō wa ku-ji ni ginkō ni itte, jū-ji ni depāto ni itte, go-ji ni kaerimashita.** (kee-nohh wah koo-jee nee geen-kohh nee eet-teh, jooo-jee nee deh-pahh-toh nee eet-teh, goh-jee nee kah-eh-ree-mah-shee-tah; Yesterday, I went to the bank at 9:00, went to the department store at 10:00, and went home at 5:00.)

✔ **15-nichi ni itte, 18-nichi ni kaerimasu.** (jooo-goh-nee-chee nee eet-teh, jooo-hah-chee-nee-chee nee kah-eh-ree-mah-soo; I'll go there on the 15th, and I'll be back on the 18th.)

✔ **Raigetsu Furansu ni itte, Supein ni itte, Itaria ni ikimasu.** (rah-ee-geh-tsoo foo-rahn-soo nee eet-teh, soo-peh-een nee eet-teh, ee-tah-ree-ah nee ee-kee-mah-soo; Next month I'll go to France, Spain, and Italy.)

Words to Know

karendā	kah-rehn-dahh	calendar
ryokō	ryoh-kohh	trip/travel
tabi	tah-bee	journey
toshi	toh-shee	year
tsuki	tsoo-kee	month
shū	shooo	week
hi	hee	day
yōbi	yohh-bee	day of the week

Changing with the Seasons

Does your part of the world have **shiki** (shee-kee; four seasons), or does it have only some combination of **haru** (hah-roo; spring), **natsu** (nah-tsoo; summer), **aki** (ah-kee; fall), and **fuyu** (foo-yoo; winter)?

To take advantage of the best that Japan has to offer, follow this seasonal mini-tour. In **haru**, don't miss **hanami** (hah-nah-mee; flower viewing). In **natsu**, go to the **inaka** (ee-nah-kah; countryside) for **Bon** (bohn; the Buddhist festival of the dead). In **aki**, drive around in the **yama** (yah-mah; mountains) and enjoy the **kōyō** (kohh-yohh; colored leaves). In **fuyu**, go to the **yuki matsuri** (yoo-kee mah-tsoo-ree; snow festival) in **Hokkaidō** (hohk-kah-ee-dohh) to view the magnificent snow sculptures.

Talking about the Days of the Week

Time flies. **Isshūkan** (ees-shooo-kahn; one week) is over before you know it. And the **shūmatsu** (shooo-mah-tsoo; weekend) is too short! It's always **getsuyōbi** (geh-tsoo-yohh-bee; Monday) again.

Both American and Japanese weeks have seven days. An American week starts on **nichiyōbi** (nee-chee-yohh-bee; Sunday), but a Japanese week starts on **getsuyōbi**. Table 3-10 lists the days of the week.

Table 3-10	Days of the Week	
Day	*Japanese*	*Pronunciation*
Monday	getsuyōbi	geh-tsoo-yohh-bee
Tuesday	kayōbi	kah-yohh-bee
Wednesday	suiyōbi	soo-ee-yohh-bee
Thursday	mokuyōbi	moh-koo-yohh-bee
Friday	kinyōbi	keen-yohh-bee
Saturday	doyōbi	doh-yohh-bee
Sunday	nichiyōbi	nee-chee-yohh-bee

Here are some useful phrases containing the days of the week:

✔ **Kyō wa nanyōbi desu ka.** (kyohh wah nahn-yohh-bee deh-soo kah; What day is it today?)

✔ **Kyō wa doyōbi desu.** (kyohh wah doh-yohh-bee deh-soo; Today is Saturday.)

✔ **Getsuyōbi kara kinyōbi made hatarakimasu.** (geh-tsoo-yohh-bee kah-rah keen-yohh-bee mah-deh hah-tah-rah-kee-mah-soo; I work from Monday to Friday.)

✔ **Konsāto wa doyōbi desu.** (kohn-sahh-toh wa doh-yohh-bee deh-soo; The concert is on Saturday.)

✔ **Nichiyōbi wa yukkuri shimasu.** (nee-chee-yohh-bee wah yook-koo-ree shee-mah-soo; I relax on Sundays.)

Telling Time

You can express **jikoku** (jee-koh-koo; time) in Japanese by using the counter **-ji** (jee; o'clock), as shown in Table 3-11.

Table 3-11	Time	
Japanese	*Pronunciation*	*Translation*
1-ji	ee-chee-jee	1 o'clock
2-ji	nee-jee	2 o'clock
3-ji	sahn-jee	3 o'clock
4-ji	yoh-jee	4 o'clock
5-ji	goh-jee	5 o'clock
6-ji	roh-koo-jee	6 o'clock
7-ji	shee-chee-jee	7 o'clock
8-ji	hah-chee-jee	8 o'clock
9-ji	koo-jee	9 o'clock
10-ji	jooo-jee	10 o'clock
11-ji	jooo-ee-chee-jee	11 o'clock
12-ji	jooo-nee-jee	12 o'clock

If you want to specify **gozen** (goh-zehn; a.m.) or **gogo** (goh-goh; p.m.), put the appropriate word in front of the number. Here are a couple of examples:

✔ **gozen 2-ji** (goh-zehn nee-jee; 2 a.m.)

✔ **gogo 3-san-ji 17-fun** (goh-goh sahn-jee jooo-nah-nah-foon; 3:17 p.m.)

You can use the convenient phrase **han** (hahn; half) for "half an hour" or "30 minutes." **Mae** (mah-eh; before) and **sugi** (soo-gee; after) are also convenient for telling time. Sorry, but Japanese doesn't have a simple phrase for "quarter-hour" or "15 minutes."

To ask "What time is it now?" say **Ima nan-ji desu ka** (ee-mah nahn-jee deh-soo kah). Here are some possible answers:

✔ **1-ji han** (ee-chee-jee hahn; 1:30)

✔ **2-ji 5-fun mae** (nee-jee goh-foon mah-eh; 5 minutes before 2:00)

✔ **3-ji 5-fun sugi** (sahn-jee goh-foon soo-gee; 5 minutes after 3:00)

Japanese schedules usually follow the 24-hour system. For example, **1-ji** (ee-chee-jee) means 1 a.m., and **13-ji** (jooo-sahn-jee) means 1 p.m. All you have to do is say the number and add **-ji** to the end. This system eliminates a.m./p.m. ambiguity, so you don't need to say **gozen** or **gogo**.

To ask questions like *at what time, from what time,* and *until what time,* you need the particle **ni** (nee; at), **kara** (kah-rah; from), or **made** (mah-deh; until). Make sure you place the particle after the time phrase. Grammatically speaking, Japanese is often the mirror image of English, and this is one of those times. "At 5:00" is "5:00 at" in Japanese, "from 7:00" is "7:00 from" in Japanese, and "until 9:00" is "9:00 until" in Japanese.

✔ **Nan-ji kara desu ka. Ni-ji kara desu.** (nahn-jee kah-rah deh-soo kah. nee-jee kah-rah deh-soo; From what time is it? From 2:00.)

✔ **Nan-ji made desu ka. San-ji made desu.** (nahn-jee mah-deh deh-soo kah. sahn-jee mah-deh deh-soo; Until what time is it? Until 3:00.)

✓ **Konsāto wa nan-ji ni hajimarimasu ka. San-ji ni hajimarimasu.** (kohn-sahh-toh wah nahn-jee nee hah-jee-mah-ree-mah-soo kah. sahn-jee nee hah-jee-mah-ree-mah-soo; What time does the concert start? It starts at 3:00.)

✓ **Ēga wa 11-ji kara 12-ji made desu.** (ehh-gah wah jooo-ee-chee-jee kah-rah jooo-nee-jee mah-deh deh-soo; The movie is from 11:00 to 12:00.)

If you don't need to express an exact time, you can estimate the time of day by using the following terms:

✓ **asa** (ah-sah; morning)

✓ **hiru** (hee-roo; noon)

✓ **ban** (bahn; evening)

✓ **mayonaka** (mah-yoh-nah-kah; midnight)

Words to Know

nan-ji	nahn-jee	what time
gogo	goh-goh	p.m.
gozen	goh-zehn	a.m.
-ji	jee	o'clock
han	hahn	half an hour
5-fun	goh-foon	5 minutes
10-pun	joop-poon	10 minutes
mae	mah-eh	before
sugi	soo-gee	past, after

Telling Time Relative to Now

When dealing with time, the concepts of *before* and *after*, or *previous* and *following*, are useful. Words like *next year* and *last week* are essential. Check out the expressions in Table 3-12 and start talking about time in relative terms.

Table 3-12	Relative Time Expressions	
Past	*Present*	*Future*
sakki (sahk-kee; a little while ago)	ima (ee-mah; now)	chotto ato (choht-toh ah-toh; a little bit later)
kinō (kee-nohh; yesterday)	kyō (kyohh; today)	ashita (ah-shee-tah; tomorrow)
senshū (sehn-shooo; last week)	konshū (kohn-shooo; this week)	raishū (rah-ee-shooo; next week)
sengetsu (sehn-geh-tsoo; last month)	kongetsu (kohn-geh-tsoo; this month)	raigetsu (rah-ee-geh-tsoo; next month)
kyonen (kyoh-nehn; last year)	kotoshi (koh-toh-shee; this year)	rainen (rah-ee-nehn; next year)

Money, Money, Money

This section gives you important words and phrases for acquiring and spending **o-kane** (oh-kah-neh; money).

Exchanging money

In Japan, the **en** (ehn — drop that *y* sound; yen) is the only acceptable **tsūka** (tsooo-kah; currency). You can

ryōgae suru (ryohh-gah-eh soo-roo; exchange) money
at the **kūkō** (kooo-kohh; airport) or at major **ginkō**
(geen-kohh; banks). Find the **gaika** (gah-ee-kah; foreign
currency) that you have in your pocket in Table 3-13.

Table 3-13	Currencies	
Currency	*Pronunciation*	*Translation*
Amerika doru	ah-meh-ree-kah doh-roo	U.S. dollar
Igirisu pondo	ee-gee-ree-soo pohn-doh	British pound
Kanada doru	kah-nah-dah doh-roo	Canadian dollar
Mekishiko peso	meh-kee-shee-koh peh-soh	Mexican peso
Ōsutoraria doru	ohh-soo-toh-rah-ree-ah doh-roo	Australian dollar
Yūro	yooo-roh	Euro

Ask for the current **kawase rēto** (kah-wah-seh rehh-
toh; exchange rate) and **ryōgae suru** (ryohh-gah-eh
soo-roo; exchange) your currency for **en.** Here are
some helpful phrases:

- ✓ **Gaika no ryōgae wa dekimasu ka.** (gah-ee-kah
  noh ryohh-gah-eh wah deh-kee-mah-soo kah;
  Can you exchange foreign currency?)

- ✓ **Kyō no kawase rēto o oshiete kudasai.** (kyohh
  noh kah-wah-seh rehh-toh oh oh-shee-eh-teh
  koo-dah-sah-ee; Please tell me today's exchange
  rate.)

- ✓ **Amerika doru o en ni ryōgae shi-tai-n-desu ga.**
  (ah-meh-ree-kah doh-roo oh ehn nee ryohh-gah-
  eh shee-tah-een-deh-soo gah; I'd like to exchange
  some American dollars for yen, is that okay?)

✔ **500-doru o en ni ryōgae shite kudasai.** (goh-hyah-koo-doh-roo oh ehn nee ryohh-gah-eh shee-teh koo-dah-sah-ee; Please exchange 500 dollars for yen.)

Words to Know

en	ehn	yen
doru	doh-roo	dollar
gaika	gah-ee-kah	foreign currency
genkin	gehn-keen	cash
ryōgae suru	ryohh-gah-eh soo-roo	to exchange
kawase rēto	kah-wah-seh rehh-toh	exchange rate
tesūryō	teh-sooo-ryohh	fee

Opening a bank account

If you open a **kōza** (kohh-za; account) at a **ginkō** (geen-kohh; bank), your money will be safe and you can earn **risoku** (ree-soh-koo; interest). Opening an account is convenient, too. If you run out of **o-kane** (oh-kah-neh; money), you can always ask your mother to **densō suru** (dehn-sohh soo-roo; wire) some money to your **kōza.**

To **hiraku** (hee-rah-koo; open) a **kōza** at a **ginkō**, you need **mibun shōmēsho** (mee-boon shohh-mehh-shoh; identification), as well as money for your deposit. Practice conjugating the u-verb **hiraku** (hee-rah-koo; to open). Notice the *k* in all the forms except the te-form.

Form	*Pronunciation*
hiraku	hee-rah-koo
hirakanai	hee-rah-kah-nah-ee
hiraki	hee-rah-kee
hiraite	hee-rah-ee-teh

Making deposits and withdrawals

If you have too much **genkin** (gehn-keen; cash) in your **saifu** (sah-ee-foo; wallet), go to a **ginkō** and make a **yokin** (yoh-keen; deposit). Don't make a mistake when you fill in your **kōza bangō** (kohh-zah bahn-gohh; account number), or you may make a stranger very happy.

When you run out of **genkin,** go to your **ginkō** or a **kyasshu mashīn** (kyahs-shoo mah-sheeen; ATM) and **hikidasu** (hee-kee-dah-soo; withdraw) more. All you need is your **kyasshu kādo** (kyahs-shoo kahh-doh; ATM card). You can make a **hikiotoshi** (hee-kee-oh-toh-shee; withdrawal) or **furikomi** (foo-ree-koh-mee; transfer). When you withdraw money from an ATM, you may see instructions like the following:

- ✔ **Kādo o o-ire kudasai.** (kahh-doh oh oh-ee-reh koo-dah-sah-ee; Insert your card, please.)
- ✔ **Anshō bangō o dōzo.** (ahn-shohh bahn-gohh oh dohh-zoh; Enter your PIN.)
- ✔ **Shibaraku o-machi kudasai.** (shee-bah-rah-koo oh-mah-chee koo-dah-sah-ee; Please wait.)
- ✔ **Kingaku o dōzo.** (keen-gah-koo oh dohh-zoh; Enter the amount, please.)
- ✔ **Genkin o o-uketori kudasai.** (gehn-keen oh oh-oo-keh-toh-ree koo-dah-sah-ee; Take the cash.)
- ✔ **Kādo o o-tori kudasai.** (kahh-doh oh oh-toh-ree koo-dah-sah-ee; Remove your card.)

Chapter 4

Making New Friends and Enjoying Small Talk

In This Chapter

▶ Greeting friends and strangers

▶ Saying thank you and I'm sorry

▶ Chatting with others

▶ Exchanging personal information

Communication starts by introducing yourself to new people, and making pleasant conversation strengthens relationships. This chapter is all about the language of meeting, greeting, and making friends.

Meeting and Greeting

Aisatsu (ah-ee-sah-tsoo; greetings) are important communication tools, setting the stage for a friendly encounter. In this section, I explain how to say important phrases like hello, my name is, and good-bye.

Saying hello

The first word you say when introducing yourself to someone for the first time is **hajimemashite** (hah-jee-meh-mah-shee-teh). This word literally means "beginning," and it clarifies the fact that you're meeting the person for the first time. Next, say your name and then say **yoroshiku onegaishimasu** (yoh-roh-shee-koo oh-neh-gah-ee-she-mah-soo). **Yoroshiku** is a set phrase that shows your modest attitude and asks the other person to be friendly. No English translation exists for it.

The response to **yoroshiku onegaishimasu** is usually **kochirakoso yoroshiku onegaishimasu** (koh-chee-rah-koh-soh yoh-roh-shee-koo oh-neh-gah-ee-she-mah-soo), meaning "It's I who should say that." So if you beg someone to be friendly, they beg you right back. After all that begging, you're friends!

Asking people their names

As in English, telling someone your **namae** (nah-mah-eh; name) in Japanese is more or less a cue for that person to tell you his or her name. If it doesn't turn out that way, you can ask **Shitsurei desu ga, o-namae wa** (shee-tsoo-rehh deh-soo gah, oh-nah-mah-eh wah; I may be rude, but what's your name?).

Bowing

Bowing plays a very important role in Japanese communication. Phrases expressing gratitude, apologies, and greetings are almost always accompanied by a bow. The Japanese also bow when meeting someone for the first time.

You don't need to bow very deeply in this context. Just slowly tilt your head and upper back slightly forward and hold the position for two seconds. The deep, long bow is needed only when you make a horrible mistake, receive overwhelming kindness, or associate with people to whom you must show a great deal of respect. Westerners aren't expected to bow, but if you do, you'll certainly impress and please.

Your own name is **namae,** but someone else's name is **o-namae.** The polite prefix **o-** shows respect to others. In English, the word translates to "honorable," which is why Japanese characters in B movies always say "honorable this" and "honorable that." But "honorable" is a mouthful compared to **o-,** which attaches to words much more naturally.

Sometimes, using **o-** is obligatory regardless of whether you're talking about yourself or about others. For example, the word for *money* is **kane** (kah-neh), but people almost always call it **okane** (oh-kah-neh).

Addressing friends and strangers

In English, you address others by their first names ("Hi, Robert!"), by their nicknames ("Hey, Bobby!"), by their positions ("Excuse me, professor"), or by their family names and appropriate titles ("Hello, Mr. Wright"), depending on your relationship.

In Japanese society, addressing people is something you don't want to mess up. When you meet someone new at work and you know the person's occupational title, such as company president, professor, or division manager, use the title along with his or her family name — for example, **Sumisu-shachō** (soo-mee-soo-shah-chohh; President Smith). Following are some examples of occupational titles:

- ✔ **buchō** (boo-chohh; department manager)
- ✔ **gakuchō** (gah-koo-chohh; university president)
- ✔ **kōchō** (kohh-chohh; principal)
- ✔ **sensei** (sehn-sehh; teacher)
- ✔ **shachō** (shah-chohh; company president)
- ✔ **tenchō** (tehn-chohh; store manager)

If you don't know the person's occupational title, the safest way to address him or her is to use his or her family name plus the respectful title **-san** (sahn), as in — **Sumisu-san** (soo-mee-soo-sahn; Ms. Smith). **-Sama** (sah-mah) is even more polite, but it's too formal and businesslike for most social situations.

Other titles include **-chan** (chahn) and **-kun** (koon), but they must be used carefully. Table 4-1 shows you which titles are appropriate for friends and acquaintances, with examples of various ways to address Robert and Susan Smith.

Table 4-1	**Titles**	
Title	**Function**	**Example**
-chan (chahn)	For children, used after a boy's or girl's given name.	Sūzan-chan (sooo-zahn-chahn), Robāto-chan (roh-bahh-toh-chahn)
-kun (koon)	Used after a boy's given name	Robāto-kun (roh-bahh-toh-koon)
	Also used after a subordinate's family name, regardless of gender.	Sumisu-kun (soo-mee-soo-koon)
-sama (sah-mah)	Used after a superior's or customer's name, regardless of gender. Also used when addressing letters (Dear . . .).	Sumisu-sama (soo-mee-soo-sah-mah), Sūzan-sama (sooo-zahn-sah-mah), Robāto Sumisu-sama (roh-bahh-toh soo-mee-soo-sah-mah)
-san (sahn)	The most common title used, especially when the person's relationship to you is unclear.	Sumisu-san (soo-mee-soo-sahn), Sūzan-san (sooo-zahn-sahn), Robāto Sumisu-san (roh-bahh-toh soo-mee-soo-sahn)

When introducing themselves, the Japanese give their family name first and given name second. Most Japanese people realize that Western names aren't in the same order, and they don't expect you to reverse the order of your own name to match the pattern of their names.

If you use the Japanese word for "you" — **anata** (ah-nah-tah) — you'll sound boastful or rude. Japanese uses names or titles where English uses "you." Instead of "you," you can use age- and gender-sensitive terms when addressing strangers in friendly contexts. For example, **ojisan** (oh-jee-sahn) literally means "uncle," but you can use it to address any unfamiliar middle-aged man. The following list shows other general terms you can use to address strangers:

- Middle-aged man: **ojisan** (oh-jee-sahn; literally, uncle)

- Middle-aged woman: **obasan** (oh-bah-sahn; literally, aunt)

- Old man: **ojīsan** (oh-jeee-sahn; literally, grandfather)

- Old woman: **obāsan** (oh-bahh-sahn; literally, grandmother)

- Young boy: **bōya** or **obocchan** (bohh-yah *or* oh-boht-chahn; literally, son)

- Young girl: **ojōsan** (oh-johh-sahn; literally, daughter)

- Young man: **onīsan** (oh-neee-sahn; literally, big brother)

- Young woman: **onēsan** (oh-nehh-sahn; literally, big sister)

Words to Know

Hajimemashite.	hah-jee-meh-mah-shee-teh	How do you do?
Yoroshiku.	yoh-roh-shee-koo	Pleased to meet you.
O-namae wa.	oh-nah-mah-eh wah	What's your name?
Watashi no namae wa _____ desu.	wah-tah-shee noh nah-mah-eh wah _____ deh-soo	My name is _____.

Greeting all day long

In Japanese, as in every other language, what you say and do to greet people depends on the time of the day and the person you're greeting. See Table 4-2.

Table 4-2	Greetings	
Japanese	*Pronunciation*	*Translation*
ohayō	oh-hah-yohh	good morning (informal)
ohayō gozaimasu	oh-hah-yohh goh-zah-ee-mah-soo	good morning (formal)
konnichiwa	kohn-nee-chee-wah	good afternoon
konbanwa	kohn-bahn-wah	good evening

Just saying "hi" is impolite. If you haven't seen someone for a while, ask **O-genki desu ka** (oh-gehn-kee deh-soo kah; How are you?) as well.

When others ask you how you are, you can say **Hai, genki desu** (hah-ee, gehn-kee deh-soo; I'm fine), but if you want to sound a bit more sophisticated, you can say **Hai, okagesamade** (hah-ee oh-kah-geh-sah-mah-deh; Yes, I'm fine thanks to you and God) or **Nantoka** (nahn-toh-kah; I'm barely managing things in my life *or* I'm barely coping). These two expressions sound modest and mature to the Japanese, although they sound pretty negative to American ears.

English speakers make a habit of asking everyone, friends and strangers alike, how they are, even if they know that the person is fine. Asking this question in Japanese is different. **O-genki desu ka** is a serious question about a person's mental and physical health.

Paying attention and saying so

When someone says something to you or gives you a piece of information, you can't just stare back. You must nod. You can also say **ā, sō desu ka** (ahh, sohh deh-soo kah), which means "Oh, really?" or "Oh, I see." Or you can just say **ā** (ahh) as you nod to convey the same message. By doing so, you acknowledge the information given. If you don't do it, your conversation partner may begin to think that you're upset or rude.

Saying good-bye

When you leave a friend, say **jā, mata** (jahh mah-tah; see you again). If you're parting for a longer period, you can also say **sayōnara** (sah-yohh-nah-rah; good-bye), but don't use this option if you'll see the person later the same day.

When you bid farewell to your boss or teacher, say **shitsurei shimasu** (shee-tsoo-rehh-shee-mah-soo). **Shitsurei shimasu** literally means "I'll be rude." How do you get "good-bye" out of "I'll be rude"? It's as if you're saying "I'm being rude by leaving your presence."

Never say **sayōnara** to your family members when you leave for school or work. It sounds like you'll never be back. Instead, say **ittemairimasu** (eet-teh-mah-ee-ree-mah-soo; literally, I'll go and come back).

Expressing Gratitude and Regret

Phrases of gratitude and apology are the most essential phrases in any language. Suppose a stranger holds a door open for you when you're entering a building. What do you say? Suppose you accidentally step on someone's foot. How do you say "I'm sorry"?

You may know the word **arigatō** (ah-ree-gah-tohh; thanks), but you may not know that you use it only when speaking to family, friends, coworkers, subordinates, or strangers who appear easygoing and younger than you. When thanking a teacher, boss, stranger who looks older than you, or stranger who looks as if he or she isn't so easygoing, say one of the following phrases instead:

- ✔ **Dōmo arigato gozaimasu.** (dohh-moh ah-ree-gah-tohh goh-zah-ee-mah-soo; Thank you, very formal)

- ✔ **Arigatō gozaimasu.** (ah-ree-gah-tohh-goh-zah-ee-mah-soo; Thank you, formal)

- ✔ **Dōmo.** (dohh-moh; Thank you, informal)

The easiest phrase of gratitude is **dōmo** — an adverb that literally means "indeed" or "very much" but can be understood as "thank you." You can use this short, convenient, yet polite phrase of gratitude in any context. If you want to express a greater-than-normal degree of gratitude, use one of the longer phrases.

To reply to a compliment, say **Dōmo** (dohh-moh; Thank you) or choose one of the following modest phrases:

- ✔ **Īe, heta desu.** (eee-eh, heh-tah deh-soo; No, I'm bad.)

✔ **Īe, madamada desu.** (eee-eh, mah-dah-mah-dah deh-soo; No, not yet, not yet.)

✔ **Īe, zenzen.** (eee-eh, zehn-zehn; No, not at all.)

To apologize for something you've done or for causing someone pain or inconvenience, say **Dōmo sumimasen** (dohh-moh soo-mee-mah-sehn; I'm very sorry). In an informal context, **Gomennasai** (goh-mehn-nah-sah-ee; Sorry) is just fine.

Making Small Talk

Small talk helps people get to know one another. This section presents some common small-talk topics.

Breaking the ice and asking questions

Small talk usually starts with **sumimasen** (soo-mee-mah-sehn; excuse me). You use this word to break the ice.

Then you usually need to ask a few questions to strike up a conversation. If you can form a sentence, you can easily form a question in Japanese. Unlike in English, you don't have to invert the subject and the verb when you ask a question in Japanese.

How you form a question depends on the answer you're expecting. Are you expecting "yes" or "no," or are you expecting a specific piece of information, like a name, place, or date?

To form a yes/no question, just add the question particle **ka** (kah) at the end of the statement and use a rising intonation, as you do in English. (See Chapter 2 for more on particles.) For example:

✔ **Jon wa kimasu** (john wah kee-mah-soo) means "John will come."

✔ **Jon wa kimasu ka** (john wah kee-mah-soo kah) means "Will John come?"

To ask a question that expects specific information in response, use a question word in addition to the particle **ka** at the end of the sentence. Just like in English, different question words are used depending on what's being asked, as shown in Table 4-3.

Table 4-3	Question Words	
Question Word	*Pronunciation*	*Translation*
dare	dah-ree	who (informal)
doko	doh-koh	where
donata	doh-nah-tah	who (formal)
dore	doh-reh	which one
dō	dohh	how
ikura	ee-koo-rah	how much
itsu	ee-tsoo	when
nani	nah-nee	what

You can use these simple ice-breaking questions to make small talk:

- ✔ **Doko ni ikimasu ka.** (doh-koh nee ee-kee-mah-soo kah; Where are you going?)

- ✔ **Ima, nan-ji desu ka.** (ee-mah, nahn-jee deh-soo kah; What time is it now?)

- ✔ **Mein Sutorīto wa doko desu ka.** (meh-een soo-toh-reee-toh wah doh-koh deh-soo kah; Where is Main Street?)

Talking about the weather

The **tenki** (tehn-kee; weather) is a universally neutral topic. On a clear day, try starting a conversation with **Ii tenki desu ne** (eee tehn-kee deh-soo neh; It's nice today, isn't it?). The following adjectives describe temperature and humidity:

- **atatakai** (ah-tah-tah-kah-ee; warm)
- **atsui** (ah-tsoo-ee; hot)
- **mushi-atsui** (moo-shee-ah-tsoo-ee; muggy)
- **samui** (sah-moo-ee; cold)
- **suzushii** (soo-zoo-sheee; cool)

In a polite/neutral or formal context, add **desu** (deh-soo; to be) to the end of the adjective. Adjectives always sound polite when they end in **desu**. For example, you can say **Atsui desu** (ah-tsoo-ee deh-soo; It's hot) or **Atsui desu ne** (ah-tsoo-ee deh-soo neh; It's hot, isn't it?).

You can also work these nouns into weather-related conversations:

- **ame** (ah-meh; rain)
- **arashi** (ah-rah-shee; storm)
- **hare** (hah-reh; clear sky)
- **kumori** (koo-moh-ree; cloudy sky)
- **yuki** (yoo-kee; snow)

Asking people where they're from

To ask "Where are you from?" say **Dochira kara desu ka** (doh-chee-rah kah-rah deh-soo kah). **Dochira** is the polite form of **doko** (doh-koh; where), and the particle **kara** means "from."

To answer this question, replace **dochira** with a place name and eliminate the question particle **ka**. Take a look at these examples:

- **Watashi wa San Furanshisuko kara desu.** (wah-tah-shee wah sahn-foo-rahn-shee-soo-koh kah-rah deh-soo; I'm from San Francisco.)
- **Boku wa Tōkyō kara desu.** (boh-koo wah tohh-kyohh kah-rah deh-soo; I am from Tokyo.)

The second speaker uses **boku** (boh-koo) instead of **watashi** (wah-tah-shee) when referring to himself. Men and boys often substitute **boku** for **watashi** to make the sentence less formal.

To say that you live somewhere, use the te-form of the u-verb **sumu** (soo-moo; to live/reside) and add the verb **iru** (ee-roo; to exist) right after it. For example, **Tōkyō ni sunde iru** (tohh-kyohh nee soon-deh ee-roo) and its polite version, **Tōkyō ni sunde imasu** (tohh-kyohh nee soon-deh ee-mah-soo), both mean "I live in Tokyo."

Form	Pronunciation
sumu	soo-moo
sumanai	soo-mah-nah-ee
sumi	soo-mee
sunde	soon-deh

Talking about where you're going

When you strike up a conversation while traveling, talking about where you're from is usually followed by questions about where you're going. Asking someone where he or she is going is easy. Just replace the particle **kara** (kah-rah; from) in **Dochira kara desu ka** (doh-chee-rah kah-rah deh-soo kah; Where are you from?) with **made** (mah-deh; up to), and you get **Dochira made desu ka,** which means "Where are you heading to?"

When someone asks you where you're going, you could say **Sapporo made desu.** (sahp-poh-roh mah-deh deh-soo; To Sapporo.)

Talking about your family

Table 4-4 contains terms for family members. For each English term, two Japanese terms correspond — a polite term and a plain one. Which term you use depends on the context.

✔ When you refer to someone else's family, use the polite term.

✔ To talk about your own family members to people outside the family, use the plain term.

✔ When you talk to older family members (other than your spouse) or when you talk about them in an informal way, use a polite term.

For example, you can call your mother by saying **Okāsan! Doko** (oh-kahh-sahn doh-koh; Mom! Where are you?). Or you can ask your mom **Okāsan, otōsan wa doko** (oh-kahh-sahn, oh-tohh-sahn wah doh-koh; Mom, where is Dad?).

Table 4-4	Family Terms	
English	*Polite Term*	*Plain Term*
family	gokazoku (goh-kah-zoh-koo)	kazoku (kah-zoh-koo)
siblings	gokyōdai (goh-kyohh-dah-ee)	kyōdai (kyohh-dah-ee)
parents	goryōshin (goh-ryohh-sheen)	ryōshin (ryohh-sheen)
father	otōsan (oh-tohh-sahn)	chichi (chee-chee)
mother	okāsan (oh-kahh-sahn)	haha (hah-hah)
older brother	onīsan (oh-neee-sahn)	ani (ah-nee)
older sister	onēsan (oh-nehh-sahn)	ane (ah-neh)
younger brother	otōto-san (oh-tohh-toh-sahn)	otōto (oh-tohh-toh)
younger sister	imōto-san (ee-mohh-toh-sahn)	imōto (ee-mohh-toh)

(continued)

Table 4-4 *(continued)*

English	Polite Term	Plain Term
husband	goshujin (goh-shoo-jeen)	shujin (shoo-jeen)
wife	okusan (oh-koo-sahn)	kanai (kah-nah-ee)
child	kodomo-san (koh-doh-moh-sahn)	kodomo (koh-doh-moh)
son	musuko-san (moo-soo-koh-sahn)	musuko (moo-soo-koh)
daughter	musume-san (moo-soo-meh-sahn)	musume (moo-soo-meh)
grandfather	ojīsan (oh-jeee-sahn)	sofu (soh-foo)
grandmother	obāsan (oh-bahh-sahn)	sobo (soh-boh)
uncle	ojisan (oh-jee-sahn)	oji (oh-jee)
aunt	obasan (oh-bah-sahn)	oba (oh-bah)

Existing and possessing: The verbs iru and aru

To tell someone that you have or possess something, use the verbs **iru** (ee-roo) and **aru** (ah-roo). Both mean "to exist," which shows possession in Japanese. You choose the verb according to whether the item you possess is animate or inanimate:

> ✔ **Iru** shows possession of animate items, such as people and animals.

> ✔ **Aru** is for inanimate items, such as books, money, plants, and houses.

So "I have a boyfriend" is **Watashi wa bōifurendo ga iru** (wah-tah-shee wah bohh-ee-foo-rehn-doh gah ee-roo), which literally means "As for me, a boyfriend exists." Similarly, "Alison has money" is **Alison wa okane ga aru** (ah-ree-sohn wah oh-kah-neh gah ah-roo), which literally means "As for Alison, money exists."

Don't forget to put the particle **ga** at the end of the object or animal you're claiming. This particle tells the listener what the subject of your sentence is.

When speaking in a polite/neutral context, use the polite form of these verbs, **imasu** (ee-mah-soo) and **arimasu** (ah-ree-mah-soo), both of which are conjugated here. **Iru** is a ru-verb, but **aru** is slightly irregular; pay close attention to the negative form.

Form	*Pronunciation*
iru	ee-roo
inai	ee-nah-ee
i	ee
ite	ee-teh

Form	*Pronunciation*
aru	ah-roo
nai	nah-ee
ari	ah-ree
atte	aht-teh

Here are a few examples of having and not having:

> ✔ **Hima ga arimasen.** (hee-mah gah ah-ree-mah-sehn; I don't have free time.)

> ✔ **Petto ga imasu.** (peht-toh gah ee-mah-soo; I have a pet.)

✔ **Watashi wa kyōdai ga imasen.** (wah-tah-shee wah kyohh-dah-ee gah ee-mah-sehn; I don't have siblings.)

✔ **Chichi wa o-kane ga arimasu.** (chee-chee wah oh-kah-neh gah ah-ree-mah-soo; My father has money.)

Talking about your regular activities

To express that you do something regularly — run, play tennis, go to work, and so on — use the verb that expresses the activity and the verb **iru** (ee-roo; to exist), in that order. Make sure to conjugate the verb that expresses the action in the te-form. (See Chapter 2 for details on the te-form.) You can leave the verb **iru** as it is or put it in the polite form, **imasu** (ee-mah-soo).

For example, you can combine the verbs **hashiru** (hah-shee-roo; to run) and **iru** to get **hashitte iru** (hah-sheet-teh ee-roo) or **hashitte imasu** (hah-sheet-teh ee-mah-soo). Both phrases mean that someone runs regularly, sort of like saying, "I run and exist every day."

Be careful: **hashitte iru** can also be interpreted as "I'm in the middle of running." Which meaning the phrase takes on depends on the context. If you say **mainichi** (mah-ee-nee-chee; every day) before saying **hashitte imasu,** you obviously mean a regular activity: "I run every day." If you say **ima** (ee-mah; now), you mean "I'm in the middle of running now." The following sentences express regular actions:

✔ **Ken wa mainichi piza o tabete imasu.** (kehn wah mah-ee-nee-chee pee-zah oh tah-beh-teh ee-mah-soo; Ken eats pizza every day.)

✔ **Otōto wa kyonen kara daigaku ni itte imasu.** (oh-tohh-toh wah kyoh-nehn kah-rah dah-ee-gah-koo nee eet-teh ee-mah-soo; My younger brother has been going to college since last year.)

✔ **Otōsan wa itsumo nete iru yo.** (oh-tohh-sahn wah ee-tsoo-moh neh-teh ee-roo yoh; My dad is always sleeping.)

✔ **Shujin wa maishū tenisu o shite imasu.** (shoo-jeen wah mah-ee-shooo teh-nee-soo oh shee-teh ee-mah-soo; My husband plays tennis every week.)

Giving out your contact information

After chatting with someone, you may want to contact him or her. Table 4-5 lists the information you may want to collect.

Table 4-5	Contact Information	
Japanese	*Pronunciation*	*Translation*
jūsho	jooo-shoh	address
denwa bangō	dehn-wah bahn-gohh	phone number
denshi mēru adoresu	dehn-shee mehh-roo ah-doh-reh-soo	e-mail address
fakkusu bangō	fahk-koo-soo bahn-gohh	fax number

Exchanging **meishi** (mehh-shee; business cards) is also a good idea. These phrases are useful when exchanging contact information:

✔ **Denshi mēru de renraku shimasu.** (dehn-shee mehh-roo deh rehn-rah-koo shee-mah-soo; I'll contact you via e-mail.)

✔ **Denwa bangō wa nan desu ka.** (dehn-wah bahn-gohh wah nahn deh-soo kah; What's your telephone number?)

✔ **Denwa o shite kudasai.** (dehn-wah oh shee-teh koo-dah-sah-ee; Please call me.)

✔ **Jūsho o oshiete kudasai.** (jooo-shoh oh oh-shee-eh-teh koo-dah-sah-ee; Please tell me your address.)

✔ **Kore wa watashi no meishi desu.** (koh-reh wah wah-tah-shee noh mehh-shee deh-soo; This is my business card.)

✔ **Yokattara, renraku kudasai.** (yoh-kaht-tah-rah, rehn-rah-koo koo-dah-sah-ee; Get in touch if you like.)

Chapter 5

Enjoying a Drink and a Snack (or Meal)

In This Chapter

▶ Eating breakfast and lunch

▶ Going to a restaurant

▶ Talking about what you like and don't like

▶ Minding your manners

Tabemono (tah-beh-moh-noh; food) always makes people happy. Trying authentic Japanese cuisine is something you can do in any large city today. Delicate taste, artistic presentation, fresh ingredients, an appreciation of nature, and the hospitality of the person who cooks are the guiding principles of **nihon ryōri** (nee-hohn ryohh-ree; Japanese cuisine). This chapter gives you useful phrases and tips to enjoy a meal. **Tabemashō** (tah-beh-mah-shohh; Let's eat!).

Making the Most of Breakfast and Lunch

How many times a day do you eat a **shokuji** (shoh-koo-jee; meal)? If you're lucky, you **taberu** (tah-beh-roo; eat) three times a day. If you're too busy, you may eat only once or twice. If you're obsessed with food, you may eat all the time.

Japanese doesn't have one convenient adjective like
"hungry." To express hunger, you say **onaka ga suita**
(oh-nah-kah gah soo-ee-tah) or, with the polite suffix,
onaka ga sukimashita (oh-nah-kah gah soo-kee-mah-
shee-tah). **Onaka** means "belly" or "stomach," and
suita and **sukimashita** mean "became empty." You're
saying that your stomach became empty.

The following are typical **shokuji** (shoh-koo-jee; meals)
and **oyatsu** (oh-yah-tsoo; snacks):

- **asagohan/chōshoku** (ah-sah-goh-hahn/chohh-
  shoh-koo; breakfast)

- **hirugohan/chūshoku** (hee-roo-goh-hahn/chooo-
  shoh-koo; lunch)

- **bangohan/yūshoku** (bahn-goh-hahn/yooo-shoh-
  koo; supper)

- **yashoku** (yah-shoh-koo; midnight snack)

It's no accident that **shoku** appears in several of the words related to eating. This word
stem often (though not always) means "eat."

Here's how to conjugate the important u- verbs **taberu**
(tah-beh-roo; to eat) and **nomu** (noh-moo; to drink).

Form	*Pronunciation*
taberu	tah-beh-roo
tabenai	tah-beh-nah-ee
tabe	tah-beh
tabete	tah-beh-teh

Form	*Pronunciation*
nomu	noh-moo
nomanai	noh-mah-nah-ee
nomi	noh-mee
nonde	nohn-deh

Eating breakfast in two cultures

A Japanese **asagohan** (ah-sah-goh-hahn; breakfast) can be downright exquisite if you have the eyes (and the palate) to see it that way. Before stepping into a Japanese-style **shokudō** (shoh-koo-dohh; dining room) for breakfast, familiarize yourself with what they serve:

- ✔ **gohan** (goh-hahn; cooked rice)

- ✔ **hōrensō no ohitashi** (hohh-rehn-sohh noh oh-hee-tah-shee; boiled spinach seasoned with soy sauce)

- ✔ **misoshiru** (mee-soh-shee-roo; soybean-paste soup)

- ✔ **nama tamago** (nah-mah tah-mah-goh; raw eggs)

- ✔ **nattō** (naht-tohh; fermented soybeans)

- ✔ **nori** (noh-ree; seaweed)

- ✔ **onsen tamago** (ohn-sehn tah-mah-goh; hot-spring boiled egg/soft-boiled egg)

- ✔ **tsukemono** (tsoo-keh-moh-noh; pickled vegetables)

- ✔ **yakizakana** (yah-kee-zah-kah-nah; grilled/broiled fish)

You may prefer to experiment later in the day and just enjoy a Western-style breakfast. I never miss out on my morning **kōhī** (kohh-heee; coffee), and I haven't skipped my breakfast **bēguru** (behh-goo-roo; bagel) and **kurīmu chīzu** (koo-reee-moo cheee-zoo; cream cheese) for ten years. What are your favorite breakfast foods?

- ✔ **bēkon** (behh-kohn; bacon)

- ✔ **hamu** (hah-moo; ham)

- ✔ **sōsēji** (sohh-sehh-jee; sausage)

- ✔ **medamayaki** (meh-dah-mah-yah-kee; fried egg)

- ✔ **sukuranburu eggu** (soo-koo-rahn-boo-roo ehg-goo; scrambled eggs)

- **kurowassan** (koo-roh-wahs-sahn; croissant)
- **tōsuto** (tohh-soo-toh; toast)
- **jamu** (jah-moo; jam)
- **batā** (bah-tahh; butter)
- **kōcha** (kohh-chah; black tea)
- **miruku** (mee-roo-koo; milk)
- **orenji jūsu** (oh-rehn-jee jooo-soo; orange juice)

Munching your lunch

In Japan, noodles are popular lunchtime meals. The thick, white noodles that you may have seen in soups are **udon** (oo-dohn); buckwheat noodles are **soba** (soh-bah). And don't forget **rāmen** (rahh-mehn) noodles, which the Japanese adopted from China.

Rice dishes in big bowls with different toppings are also popular for lunch. These meals are called **donburi** (dohn-boo-ree; big bowl).

What do you eat for lunch?

- **hanbāgā** (hahn-bahh-gahh; hamburger)
- **piza** (pee-zah; pizza)
- **sandoicchi** (sahn-doh-eet-chee; sandwich)
- **sarada** (sah-rah-dah; salad)
- **supagettī** (soo-pah-geht-teee; spaghetti)
- **sūpu** (sooo-poo; soup)

I usually use these tasty items to give my **sandoicchi** a little kick:

- **chīzu** (cheee-zoo; cheese)
- **kechappu** (keh-chahp-poo; ketchup)
- **masutādo** (mah-soo-tahh-doh; mustard)
- **mayonēzu** (mah-yoh-nehh-zoo; mayonnaise)
- **pikurusu** (pee-koo-roo-soo; pickle)

Dining Out

You can find American-style fast-food restaurants all over the world — even in Japan. This section gives you not only fast-food words, but also the words you need to have an elegant meal in a restaurant.

Ordering fast food

Whether you're ordering **piza** (pee-zah; pizza) with friends or grabbing a **sandoicchi** (sahn-doh-eet-chee; sandwich) for lunch, you probably spend a fair amount of money enriching fast-food chains. This section tells you how to **chūmon suru** (chooo-mohn soo-roo; order) a **hanbāgā** (hahn-bahh-gahh; hamburger) and **furaido poteto** (foo-rah-ee-doh poh-teh-toh; fries) in Japanese. Check out some other popular fast-food dishes:

- ✔ **chikin bāgā** (chee-keen bahh-gahh; chicken patty)
- ✔ **chīzu bāgā** (cheee-zoo bahh-gahh; cheeseburger)
- ✔ **furaido chikin** (foo-rah-ee-doh chee-keen; fried chicken)
- ✔ **hotto doggu** (hoht-toh dohg-goo; hot dog)
- ✔ **miruku shēku** (mee-roo-koo shehh-koo; milkshakes)

Now that you have a handle on the menu, practice conjugating the verb **chūmon suru** (chooo-mohn soo-roo; to order). This term is actually a combination of the noun **chūmon** (order) and the verb **suru** (to do), so you conjugate just the **suru** part. Yes, it's an irregular verb.

Form	Pronunciation
chūmon suru	chooo-mohn soo-roo
chūmon shinai	chooo-mohn shee-nah-ee
chūmon shi	chooo-mohn shee
chūmon shite	chooo-mohn shee-teh

You may have to answer a couple of questions when you order at a fast-food joint:

- ✔ **Omochi kaeri desu ka** (oh-moh-chee kah-eh-ree deh-soo kah) means "Will you take it home?" or "To go?"

- ✔ **Kochira de omeshiagari desu ka** (koh-chee-rah deh oh-meh-shee-ah-gah-ree deh-soo kah) means "Will you eat here?" or "For here?"

If you hear one of these questions, just answer **hai** (hah-ee; yes) or **īe** (eee-eh; no).

Making dinner reservations

The Japanese are gourmets. They often line up in front of popular restaurants, and they don't mind waiting an hour or more. If you don't want to wait in line, make a **yoyaku** (yoh-yah-koo; reservation) over the phone.

The Japanese say "to make a reservation" by saying "to do a reservation," which is **yoyaku o suru** (yoh-yah-koo oh soo-roo). Remember that **suru** (soo-roo; to do) is an irregular verb.

Conjugate **yoyaku o suru.** Because **yoyaku** is a noun, all you have to worry about is the **suru** part.

Form	Pronunciation
yoyaku o suru	yoh-yah-koo oh soo-roo
yoyaku o shinai	yoh-yah-koo oh shee-nah-ee
yoyaku o shi	yoh-yah-koo oh shee
yoyaku o shite	yoh-yah-koo oh shee-teh

First, tell the restaurant's host when you want to arrive. (Chapter 3 explains the basics of how to tell time in Japanese, including the concepts of a.m., p.m., and o'clock.) Table 5-1 provides the time ranges you're likely to need when making dinner reservations.

Table 5-1	A Timetable	
Time	**Japanese**	**Pronunciation**
6:00	roku-ji	roh-koo-jee
6:15	roku-ji jūgo-fun	roh-koo-jee jooo-goh-foon
6:30	roku-ji han	roh-koo-jee hahn
6:45	roku-ji yonjūgo-fun	roh-koo-jee yohn-jooo-goh-foon
7:00	shichi-ji	shee-chee-jee
8:00	hachi-ji	hah-chee-jee
9:00	ku-ji	koo-jee

When you talk about an approximate time, add **goro** (goh-roh) after the time phrase. **Roku-ji goro** (roh-koo-jee goh-roh), for example, means "about 6:00."

After you establish a time, let the host know how many people are in your party. Japanese uses a _counter_ (a short suffix that follows a number) to count people. Which counter you use depends on the item you're counting. For example, you can't just say **go** (goh; five) when you have five people in your party. You have to say **go-nin** (goh-neen), because **-nin** (neen) is the counter for people. But watch out for the irregular **hitori** (hee-toh-ree; one person) and **futari** (foo-tah-ree; two people).

Table 5-2 can help you count people.

Table 5-2   Expressing a Number of People

Number of People	Japanese	Pronunciation
1	hitori	hee-toh-ree
2	futari	foo-tah-ree
3	san-nin	sahn-neen
4	yo-nin	yoh-neen
5	go-nin	goh-neen
6	roku-nin	roh-koo-neen
7	nana-nin	nah-nah-neen
8	hachi-nin	hah-chee-neen
9	kyū-nin	kyooo-neen
10	jū-nin	jooo-neen

Here's how a typical conversation about a restaurant reservation may go:

Host: **Maido arigatō gozaimasu.** (mah-ee-doh ah-ree-gah-tohh goh-zah-ee-mah-soo; Thank you for your patronage. How can I help you?)

Makoto: **Anō, konban, yoyaku o shitai-n-desu ga.** (ah-nohh, kohn-bahn, yoh-yah-koo oh shee-tah-een-deh-soo gah; I would like to make a reservation for tonight.)

Host: **Hai, arigatō gozaimasu. Nan-ji goro.** (hah-ee, ah-ree-gah-tohh goh-zah-ee-mah-soo. nahn-jee goh-roh; Yes, thank you. About what time?)

Makoto: **Shichi-ji desu.** (shee-chee-jee deh-soo; 7:00, please.)

Host: **Hai. Nan-nin-sama.** (hah-ee. nahn-neen-sah-mah; Certainly. How many people?)

Makoto: **Go-nin desu.** (goh-neen deh-soo; Five people.)

In Japanese, you often form a statement by using **-n-desu** (n-deh-soo) in conversation. The effect of **-n-desu** is to encourage your partner to respond. Saying **Yoyaku o shitai-n-desu** (yoh-yah-koo oh shee-tah-een-deh-soo; I'd like to make a reservation) sounds much more inviting and friendly than saying **Yoyaku o shitai desu** because it shows your willingness to listen to the other person's comments.

Use **-n-desu** in informal conversation but not in writing or public speech.

When you follow a verb with **-n-desu,** the verb must be in the informal/plain form. Ending your statement with the particle **ga** (gah; but), as in **Yoyaku o shitai-n-desu ga,** makes it clear that you're waiting for the other person to reply.

Ordering in a restaurant

How do you order in a restaurant? Do you carefully go over the **menyū** (meh-nyooo; menu), or do you look to see what other people are eating? Do you ask the **uētā** (oo-ehh-tahh; waiter) or **uētoresu** (oo-ehh-toh-reh-soo; waitress) for direction as to what's good? Do you routinely order a **zensai** (zehn-sah-ee; appetizer), an **o-nomimono** (oh-noh-mee-moh-noh; beverage), and a **dezāto** (deh-zahh-toh; dessert) in addition to your entrée? In this section, I provide you with phrases and concepts that you need to order in a restaurant.

Whether you go to a four-star restaurant or the corner pub, your waiter or waitress will ask you questions like these:

- ✔ **Gochūmon wa.** (goh-chooo-mohn wah; Your order?)

- ✔ **Nani ni nasaimasu ka.** (nah-nee nee nah-sah-ee-mah-soo kah; What will you have?)

- ✔ **O-nomimono wa.** (oh-noh-mee-moh-noh wah; Anything to drink?)

Here are a few phrases that you can use when talking to the waitstaff:

- ✔ **Rāmen o mittsu onegaishimasu.** (rahh-mehn oh meet-tsoo oh-neh-gah-ee-shee-mah-soo; Can we have ramen noodles for three please?)

- ✔ **Sushi to sashimi to misoshiru o onegaishimasu.** (soo-shee toh sah-shee-mee toh mee-soh-shee-roo oh oh-neh-gah-ee-shee-mah-soo; Can I have sushi, sashimi, and miso soup please?)

- ✔ **Wain wa arimasu ka.** (wah-een wah ah-ree-mah-soo kah; Do you have wine?)

- ✔ **Osusumehin wa?** (oh-soo-soo-meh-hin wah; What do you recommend?)

To list several dishes, use **to** (toh) between dishes to link them. (Think of **to** as a verbal comma or the word *and*.) To specify the quantity of each item you want to order, use the counter that applies to food items, **-tsu:**

- ✔ **hito-tsu** (hee-toh-tsoo; one food item)
- ✔ **futa-tsu** (foo-tah-tsoo; two food items)
- ✔ **mit-tsu** (meet-tsoo; three food items)

If you can't read the menu at a Japanese restaurant, don't worry. Most restaurants in Japan have colored pictures on the menu or life-sized wax models of the food in their windows. The easiest way to order is to follow this simple formula: Point to the picture of the dish on the menu, say **kore o** (koh-reh oh; this one), and say **onegaishimasu** (oh-neh-gah-ee-shee-mah-soo; I'd like to ask you) or **kudasai** (koo-dah-sah-ee; please give me) at the end.

Do you see any of your favorites on this dinner menu?

- ✔ **bifuteki** (bee-foo-teh-kee; beef steak)
- ✔ **bīfu shichū** (beee-foo shee-chooo; beef stew)

- ✔ **masshu poteto** (mas-shoo poh-teh-toh; mashed potato)
- ✔ **mīto rōfu** (meee-toh rohh-foo; meatloaf)
- ✔ **pan** (pahn; bread)
- ✔ **sake** (sah-keh; salmon)
- ✔ **sarada** (sah-rah-dah; salad)
- ✔ **sūpu** (sooo-poo; soup)

Which of the following Japanese dishes would you like to try?

- ✔ **gyūdon** (gyooo-dohn; a bowl of rice topped with cooked beef and vegetables)
- ✔ **oyako donburi** (oh-yah-koh dohn-boo-ree; a bowl of rice topped with cooked chicken and eggs)
- ✔ **shabushabu** (shah-boo-shah-boo; beef and vegetables cooked in a pot of boiling broth)
- ✔ **sukiyaki** [soo-kee-yah-kee; beef and vegetables cooked in **warishita** (wah-ree-shee-tah; a mixture of soy sauce, sugar, and liquor)]
- ✔ **tempura** (tehm-poo-rah; deep-fried vegetables or seafood)
- ✔ **unagi** (oo-nah-gee; eel)
- ✔ **yakiniku** (yah-kee-nee-koo; Korean-style barbecue)
- ✔ **yosenabe** (yoh-seh-nah-beh; Japanese casserole of vegetables, fish, or meat)

If you want to have a complete meal that comes with rice, soup, and a salad, order a **tēshoku** (tehh-shoh-koo; set meal), like **sashimi tēshoku** and **tempura tēshoku**.

Setting your table

If there's anything missing on your table, ask the waiter for it. Table 5-3 lists some items that might be missing.

Table 5-3	Dining Utensils	
Japanese	**Pronunciation**	**Translation**
fōku	fohh-koo	fork
gurasu	goo-rah-soo	glass
kappu	kahp-poo	cup
naifu	nah-ee-foo	knife
napukin	nah-poo-keen	napkin
o-sara	oh-sah-rah	plate
supūn	soo-pooon	spoon

If you're having Japanese food, you may need some of
these items:

- ✔ **hashi** (hah-shee; chopsticks)
- ✔ **o-chawan** (oh-chah-wahn; rice bowl)
- ✔ **o-wan** (oh-wahn; lacquered soup bowl)

Chatting with the waiter or waitress

Ask questions of your **uētā** (oo-ehh-tahh; waiter) or
uētoresu (oo-ehh-toh-reh-soo; waitress), or just chat
with them about the food they served.

- ✔ **Kore wa nan desu ka.** (koh-reh wah nahn deh-
  soo kah; What is this?)
- ✔ **Watashi wa ebi ga taberaremasen.** (wah-tah-
  shee wah eh-bee gah tah-beh-rah-reh-mah-sehn;
  I can't eat shrimp.)
- ✔ **Kore wa yakete imasu ka.** (koh-reh wah yah-
  keh-teh ee-mah-soo kah; Is it well done?)
- ✔ **Oishii desu ne.** (oh-ee-sheee deh-soo neh; This
  is delicious, isn't it?)
- ✔ **Chotto hen na aji desu.** (choh-toh hehn-nah ah-
  jee-deh-soo; It tastes sort of strange.)

- ✔ **Totemo oishikatta desu.** (toh-teh-moh oh-ee-shee-kaht-tah deh-soo; That was very delicious!)
- ✔ **Omizu o kudasai.** (oh-mee-zoo oh koo-dah-sah-ee; Water, please.)
- ✔ **Toire wa doko desu ka.** (toh-ee-ree wah doh-koh deh-soo kah; Where is the bathroom?)

Paying for your meal

When you eat with your friends, do you **warikan ni suru** (wah-ree-kahn nee soo-roo; go Dutch), or does one person **ogoru** (oh-goh-roo; treat) everyone? How about when you eat with your boss? He or she probably pays, but it never hurts to say **O-kanjō o onegaishimasu** (oh-kahn-johh oh oh-neh-gah-ee-shee-mah-soo; Check please), especially if you know that your boss won't let you pay.

The following phrases are handy when you pay for your meal:

- ✔ **Betsubetsu ni onegaishimasu.** (beh-tsoo-beh-tsoo nee oh-neh-gah-ee-shee-mah-soo; Please give us separate checks.)
- ✔ **Isshoni onegaishimasu.** (ees-shoh-nee oh-neh-gah-ee-shee-mah-soo); Please give us one check.)
- ✔ **O-kanjō o onegaishimasu.** (oh-kahn-johh oh oh-neh-gah-ee-shee-mah-soo; Check please.)
- ✔ **Ryōshūsho o onegaishimasu.** (ryohh-shooo-shoh oh oh-neh-gah-ee-shee-mah-soo; Receipt please.)

You don't have to tip at any restaurant in Japan, but you still get very good service 99 percent of the time. For very expensive meals, the tip is automatically included in your bill as a **sābisuryō** (sahh-bee-soo-ryohh; service charge).

Most restaurants accept **kurejitto kādo** (koo-reh-jeet-toh kahh-doh; credit cards), but many of them still only accept **genkin** (gehn-keen; cash). If you're not sure about a restaurant's policy, ask before you're seated.

Words to Know

chūmon	chooo-mohn	order
okanjō	oh-kan-johh	check, bill
kurejitto kādo	koo-reh-jeet-toh kahh-doh	credit cards
genkin	gehn-keen	cash
o-mizu	oh-mee-zoo	water
yoyaku	yoh-yah-koo	reservation

Expressing Your Likes and Dislikes

When you talk about your preferences in English, you use verbs such as *to like, to love,* and *to hate.* It may seem strange to you, but in Japanese, you use adjectives to express your likes and dislikes. For example, **suki** (soo-kee; to like) is an adjective. If you want to say that you like pizza, you say **Watashi wa piza ga suki desu** (wah-tah-shee wah pee-zah gah soo-kee deh-soo).

Express what you like in Japanese with an adjective and the particle **ga**. You can use either **ga suki** or its polite counterpart, **ga suki desu.**

If you know **suki,** you also need to know **kirai** (kee-rah-ee; to hate). If you like or hate something a lot, add **dai-** (dah-ee), which means "big," before **suki** or **kirai,** as in **daisuki** (dah-ee-soo-kee; to like it a lot) and **daikirai** (dah-ee-kee-rah-ee; to hate it a lot). Now you have four adjectives that you can use to express your likes and dislikes!

Get used to these words by reviewing the following examples:

> ✔ **Ika ga kirai desu.** (ee-kah gah kee-rah-ee deh-soo; I hate squid.)

> ✔ **Sakana ga suki desu.** (sah-kah-nah gah soo-kee deh-soo; I like fish.)

> ✔ **Watashi wa sakana ga daisuki desu.** (wah-tah-shee wah sah-kah-nah gah dah-ee-soo-kee deh-soo; I like fish a lot.)

> ✔ **Otōto wa yasai ga daikirai desu.** (oh-tohh-toh wah yah-sah-ee gah dah-ee-kee-rah-ee deh-soo; My little brother hates vegetables a lot.)

Using Proper Table Manners

When you're invited for dinner, you have to be polite. But what qualifies as polite depends on the culture and customs of your hosts. The Japanese drink soup directly from an **o-wan** (oh-wahn; Japanese lacquered soup bowl) without using a spoon. That's polite. They also slurp **ramen** noodles. That's polite, too.

When you start eating, always say **itadaki-masu** (ee-tah-dah-kee-mah-soo). It's a humble word for "receive," but it doesn't have a good English translation. Just remember that it expresses gratitude to those who prepared the meal you're about to receive. When you're done with your meal, say **gochisōsama deshita** (goh-chee-sohh-sah-mah deh-shee-tah), another word of gratitude for which there is no English equivalent.

You can also use some of these phrases at the table:

> ✔ **Oishii desu.** (oh-ee-sheee deh-soo; Delicious!)
>
> ✔ **Okawari onegaishimasu.** (oh-kah-wah-ree oh-neh-gah-ee-shee-mah-soo; May I have another serving?)
>
> ✔ **O-mizu o onegaishimasu.** (oh-mee-zoo oh oh-neh-gah-ee-shee-mah-soo; May I have some water?)

If you're the host, offer food to your guest by saying **wa ikaga** (wah ee-kah-gah; How about . . . ?). For example, you can offer mashed potatoes by saying **Masshupoteto wa ikaga desu ka** (mahs-shoo poh-teh-toh wah ee-kah-gah deh-soo kah; How about mashed potatoes?). But remember, Japanese guests tend to be shy. They often say **īe** (eee-eh; no thank you) to be polite even when they're hoping for more. Offer again by saying **go enryo shinaide** (goh ehn-ryoh shee-nah-ee-deh; Don't be shy).

Words to Know

Enryo shinaide.	ehn-ryoh shee-nah-ee-deh	Don't be shy.
Itadakimasu.	ee-tah-dah-kee-mah-soo	I'll start eating.
Oishii desu.	oh-ee-sheee deh-soo	It's delicious.
Gochisōsama deshita.	goh-chee-sohh-sah-mah deh-shee-tah	Thank you for the great meal.
okawari	oh-kah-wah-ree	another serving

Chapter 6

Shop 'til You Drop

. . . .

In This Chapter
▶ Finding the perfect outfit
▶ Negotiating the deal
▶ Coughing up the cash
▶ Shopping for groceries

. . . .

*I*f you love **kaimono** (kah-ee-moh-noh; shopping) as much as I do, grab a **kurejitto kādo** (koo-reh-jeet-toh kahh-doh; credit card) or some **genkin** (gehn-keen; cash) and get going! This chapter helps you get a handle on prices, evaluate products, and make purchases in Japanese.

Asking for a Particular Item

If you have a particular item in mind, step into a store and say **Wa arimasu ka . . .** (wah ah-ree-mah-soo kah; Do you have . . . ?). If you really want something, don't give up — continue to **sagasu** (sah-gah-soo; look for) what you want. Conjugate the u-verb **sagasu** (sah-gah-soo; look for).

Form	Pronunciation
sagasu	sah-gah-soo
sagasanai	sah-gah-sah-nah-ee
sagashi	sah-gah-shee
sagashite	sah-gah-shee-teh

If you see a nice item in a store window, ask the clerk to show it to you. Express your request by using a verb in the te-form (see Chapter 2) and **kudasai** (koo-dah-sah-ee; please), as in **Sore o misete kudasai.** (soh-reh oh mee-seh-teh koo-dah-sah-ee; Please show me that.)

How do you specify the item you want to see? You can point at it and say **kore** (koh-reh; this one), which works most of the time. But what if a **yunomi** (yoo-noh-mee; teacup) and a **kyūsu** (kyooo-soo; teapot) are right next to each other? If you say **kore,** the clerk will ask **dore** (doh-reh; which one?). You'll have to say **kore** again, and the clerk will have to say **dore** again. To end this frustrating conversation, say **kono yunomi** (koh-noh yoo-noh-mee; this teacup) or **kono kyūsu** (koh-noh kyooo-soo; this teapot). Yes, you can add a common noun to the Japanese word for *this,* but you must change **kore** to **kono.**

Similarly, **sore** (soh-reh; that one near you) and **are** (ah-reh; that one over there) become **sono** (soh-noh) and **ano** (ah-noh), respectively, when followed by a common noun. Even the question word **dore** (doh-reh; which one) must become **dono** when followed by a common noun. If you think about it, the change is systematic: The ending -**re** becomes -**no.** Check out the following examples to straighten everything out.

- ✔ **Ano biru wa nan desu ka.** (ah-noh bee-roo wah nahn deh-soo kah; What is that building?)

- ✔ **Sono nekkuresu wa takai desu ka.** (soh-noh nehk-koo-reh-soo wah tah-kah-ee deh-soo kah; Is that necklace expensive?)

Comparing Items

To find a good deal, you must carefully compare the **shōhin** (shohh-heen; merchandise). Look closely at the **hinshitsu** (heen-shee-tsoo; quality) and the **kinō** (kee-nohh; functions) of the **seihin** (sehh-heen; product) and compare several similar items.

Grammar-wise, making comparisons is much easier in Japanese than it is in English. In Japanese, you don't have to conjugate adjectives, adding *-er* or *-est* to show different degrees: **Takai** (tah-kah-ee) remains **takai** whether you want to say "expensive," "more expensive," or "most expensive."

Saying cheaper, more expensive, better, or worse

When you say "Videotapes are cheaper than DVDs," "Old furniture is better than new furniture," or "My car is more expensive than your car," you're comparing two items. In Japanese, you don't need to add *-er* or "more" to make a comparison. You just need the Japanese equivalent of "than," which is the particle **yori** (yoh-ree). Place **yori** right after the second item in the comparison.

Using the first example in this paragraph, "than DVDs" has to be "DVDs than" in Japanese. It's a mirror-image situation. Take a look at a few examples to see this concept in action:

- ✔ **Bideo tēpu wa DVD yori yasui desu.** (bee-deh-oh tehh-poo wah deee-beee-deee yoh-ree yah-soo-ee deh-soo; Videotapes are cheaper than DVDs.)

- ✔ **Furui kagu wa atarashii kagu yori ii desu.** (foo-roo-ee kah-goo wah ah-tah-rah-sheee kah-goo yoh-ree eee deh-soo; Old furniture is better than new furniture.)

- ✔ **Watashi no kuruma wa anata no kuruma yori takai desu.** (wah-tah-shee noh koo-roo-mah wah ah-nah-tah noh koo-roo-mah yoh-ree tah-kah-ee deh-soo; My car is more expensive than your car.)

Comparing two items

Life is full of comparison questions like

> ✔ Which one is better, this one or that one?
>
> ✔ Who do you like better, Mary or me?
>
> ✔ Which is more important, money or reputation?

"Which one" in Japanese is **dochira** (doh-chee-rah). Just keep in mind that **dochira** is used only when the question is about *two* items. (To find out how to ask a question about three or more items, see the section "Comparing three or more items" later in this chapter.) Here are the steps for constructing an out-of-two comparison question:

1. **List the two items you're comparing at the beginning of the sentence.**

2. **Add the particle to (toh; and) after each item to make it look like a list.**

3. **Insert the question word dochira followed by the subject-marking particle ga (gah).**

4. **Add the adjective with the question particle ka (kah).**

Did you get lost? I hope not. If you did, these examples will help clear things up:

> ✔ **Kore to, are to, dochira ga ii desu ka.** (koh-reh toh, ah-reh toh, doh-chee-rah gah eee deh-soo kah; Which one is better, this one or that one?)
>
> ✔ **Marī to, watashi to, dochira ga suki desu ka.** (mah-reee toh, wah-tah-shee toh, doh-chee-rah gah soo-kee deh-soo kah; Who do you like better, Mary or me?)
>
> ✔ **O-kane to, meisei to, dochira ga daiji desu ka.** (oh-kah-neh toh, mehh-sehh toh, doh-chee-rah gah dah-ee-jee deh-soo kah; Which one is more important, money or reputation?)

You can answer these comparison questions in a few different ways, but the simplest way is to say the item of your choice with the verb **desu** (deh-soo; to be). For example, if someone asks **Piza to, sushi to, dochira ga suki desu ka** (pee-zah toh, soo-shee toh, doh-chee-rah gah soo-kee deh-soo kah; Which one do you like better, pizza or sushi?), you can answer **piza desu** (pee-zah deh-soo; pizza) or **sushi desu** (soo-shee deh-soo; sushi).

Pointing out the best one

When shopping, you want to find the best merchandise in your budget. In Japanese, you don't need to add -*est* or "most" to adjectives to express "the best" or "the most." Just use the adverb **ichiban** (ee-chee-bahn; the most/the best). Simply place **ichiban** right before the adjective. The following examples show you how easy forming -*est* and "most" sentences in Japanese is.

> ✔ **Kono kuruma wa ichiban ōkii desu.** (koh-noh koo-roo-mah wah ee-chee-bahn ohh-keee deh-soo; This car is the biggest.)
>
> ✔ **Kono kuruma wa ichiban kōkyū desu.** (koh-noh koo-roo-mah wah ee-chee-bahn kohh-kyooo deh-soo; This car is the most luxurious.)
>
> ✔ **Kono kuruma wa ichiban yasui desu.** (koh-noh koo-roo-mah wah e-chee-bahn yah-soo-ee deh-soo; This car is the cheapest.

Comparing three or more items

To ask which item is best among three or more items listed one by one, use the question words **dare** (dah-reh), **doko** (doh-koh), and **dore** (doh-reh). Use **dare** for people, **doko** for places, and **dore** for other items, including foods, cars, animals, plants, games, and academic subjects. All three words mean "which one."

You can't use **dochira** (doh-chee-rah) to mean "which one" in this context because you use **dochira** only for a question about two items.

To ask a question comparing three or more items, list the items with the particle **to** (toh) after each item. Form the question by using the question word **dare, doko,** or **dore.** Again, **ichiban** (ee-chee-bahn; the best/most) is the key, as shown in these examples:

✔ **Besu to, Marĩ to, Jon to, dare ga ichiban yasashii desu ka.** (beh-soo toh, mah-reee toh, john toh, dah-reh gah ee-chee-bahn yah-sah-sheee deh-soo kah; Among Beth, Mary, and John, who is the kindest?)

✔ **Bosuton to, Tōkyō to, Shikago to, doko ga ichiban samui desu ka.** (boh-soo-tohn toh, tohh-kyohh toh, shee-kah-goh toh, doh-koh gah ee-chee-bahn sah-moo-ee deh-soo kah; Among Boston, Tokyo, and Chicago, which one is the coldest?)

✔ **Hanbāgā to, hotto doggu to, piza to, dore ga ichiban suki desu ka.** (hahn-bahh-gahh toh, hoht-toh dohg-goo toh, pee-zah toh, doh-reh gah ee-chee-bahn soo-kee deh-soo kah; Among hamburgers, hot dogs, and pizza, which one do you like the best?)

If you want to specify the category of the items you're comparing, like "of foods" or "among the cities in the country," specify the category at the beginning of the question and place two particles, **de** (deh) and **wa** (wah), right after it. And remember that you must use **nani** (nah-nee; what) instead of **dore** (doh-reh; which one). So if you're specifying a category rather than giving a list, use **dare** (dah-reh; who) for people, **doko** (doh-koh; where) for locations, and **nani** (nah-nee; what) for other items. Table 6-1 can help you sort things out.

Table 6-1	Saying Which One in Japanese		
Category	*Of Two Items*	*Of Three or More Items*	*Of a Category*
people	dochira	dare	dare
locations	dochira	doko	doko
other items	dochira	dore	nani

Here are a couple of "which one" questions concerning a category of items:

✔ **Nihon no machi de wa doko ga ichiban kirē desu ka.** (nee-hohn noh mah-chee deh wah doh-koh gah ee-chee-bahn kee-rehh deh-soo kah; Out of Japanese cities, which one is most beautiful?)

✔ **Tabemono de wa nani ga ichiban suki desu ka.** (tah-beh-moh-noh deh wah nah-nee gah ee-chee-bahn soo-kee deh-soo kah; Among foods, which one do you like the best?)

The simplest way to answer these questions is to use **desu** (deh-soo; to be). If someone asks you **Amerika de wa doko ga ichiban samui desu ka** (ah-meh-ree-kah deh wah doh-koh gah ee-chee-bahn sah-moo-ee deh-soo kah; Which place is the coldest in America?), you can answer **Arasuka desu** (ah-rah-soo-kah deh-soo; Alaska).

The simplest way to say "how about" is to say **wa** — the particle that designates the topic — with a rising intonation. **Wa** is the shortened form of **wa dō desu ka** (wah dohh deh-soo kah; how is). For example, a sales-person may introduce different refrigerators one by one by pointing at them and saying **kore wa.**

Shopping for Clothes

When you buy **yōfuku** (yohh-foo-koo; clothes), do you look for quality items that you can wear for ten years or more, or do you buy cheap items that you can wear for just one season? Check out Table 6-2 for a list of clothes and accessories.

Table 6-2   Articles of Clothing and Accessories

Item	Pronunciation	Translation
jaketto	jah-keht-toh	jacket
kōto	kohh-toh	coat
kutsu	koo-tsoo	shoes
kutsushita	koo-tsoo-shee-tah	socks
sētā	sehh-tahh	sweater
shatsu	shah-tsoo	shirt
shitagi	shee-tah-gee	underwear
suetto shatsu	soo-eht-toh shah-tsoo	sweatshirt
sukāto	soo-kahh-toh	skirt
zubon	zoo-bohn	pants/slacks

Asking about color

When you buy **yōfuku** (yohh-foo-koo; clothes), check out all the **iro** (ee-roh; colors) and pick the one that looks best on you.

- **aka** (ah-kah; red)
- **ao** (ah-oh; blue)
- **chairo** (chah-ee-roh; brown)
- **kīro** (keee-roh; yellow)

✔ **kuro** (koo-roh; black)

✔ **midori** (mee-doh-ree; green)

✔ **murasaki** (moo-rah-sah-kee; purple)

✔ **orenji** (oh-rehn-jee; orange)

✔ **pinku** (peen-koo; pink)

✔ **shiro** (shee-roh; white)

If the salesperson shows you a color you're not crazy about, simply ask **Chigau iro wa** (chee-gah-oo ee-roh wah; Do you have a different color?).

Using chotto for a variety of reasons

Chotto (choht-toh) is one of those wonderful words that has far more uses than a dictionary can suggest. The English translation is usually "a little," but you hear it in situations where no literal translation works. You can use **chotto** to make a request, complaint, or refusal sound understated, which makes you appear sensitive and modest — a good thing to the Japanese. Check out the many uses of **chotto:**

✔ Asking a favor: To ask a favor of someone, start with **chotto,** as in **Chotto oshiete kudasai** (choht-toh oh-shee-eh-teh koo-dah-sah-ee). This phrase translates literally as "Please teach me a little," but in more natural English, it means something like "I'd like to ask you something if I could."

✔ Asking for permission: When you need to get permission to do something, start with **chotto.** Think of the phrase **Chotto kite mite mo ii desu ka** (choht-toh kee-teh-mee-teh moh eee deh-sooo kah; literally, Can I try it on a little?) as having a meaning close to "Can I try it on for a minute?" In this context, **chotto** makes it sound as if you'll be done quickly.

Ask for permission by using the verb in the te-form (see Chapter 2) with the phrase **mo ii desu ka** (moh eee deh-soo kah). For example, **Tabete mo ii desu ka** (tah-beh-teh moh eee deh-soo kah) means "Is it okay to eat?"

  ✔ Complaining: **Chotto chīsai desu** (choht-toh
    cheee-sah-ee deh-soo; It's a little small) sounds
    gracious when everyone knows that you really
    mean "It's too small."

  ✔ Objecting: **Chotto yamete kudasai** (choht-toh
    yah-meh-teh koo-dah-sah-ee; Please stop that a
    little) sounds mild, even when you mean "Please
    stop that completely."

In many contexts, you can just say **chotto** without
completing the sentence. For example, you can say it
when you want to call your assistant to your desk, you
notice a stranger sitting on your coat, or your house-
guest asks you whether he can smoke. Saying **chotto**
brings the assistant to your desk, gets the stranger off
your coat, and tells your guest that you hate the smell
of cigarettes. Of course, you need to use the appropriate facial expressions and intonation to help convey
your meaning.

Finding the right size

If you're in a store wondering whether an article of
clothing is your **saizu** (sah-ee-zoo; size), ask the clerk
Chotto kite mite mo ii desu ka (choht-toh kee-teh
mee-teh moh eee deh-soo kah; Can I try it on a little?).
If the clerk says okay, go to the **shichakushitsu** (shee-
chah-koo-shee-tsoo; fitting room) and see whether it's
a **chōdo ii** (chohh-doh eee; exact fit). If not, you can
use one of the following phrases:

  ✔ **Chotto chīsai desu.** (choht-toh cheee-sah-ee
    deh-soo; A little small.)

  ✔ **Chotto ōkii kana.** (choht-toh ohh-keee kah-nah;
    Is it a little big for me?)

  ✔ **Nagai desu.** (nah-gah-ee deh-soo; It's long.)

  ✔ **Sukoshi mijikai desu.** (soo-koh-shee mee-jee-
    kah-ee deh-soo; A little short.)

The verb **kiru** (kee-roo; to wear) is a ru-verb. Here's
the conjugation:

Form	Pronunciaiton
kiru	kee-roo
kinai	kee-nah-ee
ki	kee
kite	kee-teh

When you want to try doing something, use the verb in the te-form and add **miru.** For example, **kite miru** (kee-teh mee-roo) means "to try wearing" or "to try on."

Trying on clothes is important, but shopping for a **T-shatsu** (teee-shah-tsoo; T-shirt) is pretty easy. You can often avoid going to the **shichakushitsu** (shee-chah-koo-shee-tsoo; fitting room) if you know your size:

- ✔ **S** (eh-soo; small)
- ✔ **M** (eh-moo; medium)
- ✔ **L** (eh-roo; large)
- ✔ **XL** (ehk-koo-soo eh-roo; extra large)

Buying a dress is more complicated. Use the counter -**gō** (gohh) when sizing up your choices. (For more on using Japanese counters, see Chapter 2.)

Women's dress sizes in Japan are one size less than they are in the United States. Here are the rough equivalents for women's dress sizes:

American	6	8	10	12	14	16
Japanese	5	7	9	11	13	15

Men's suit and coat sizes are expressed in letters in Japan. Compare American sizes and Japanese sizes:

American	34	36	38	40	42	44	46
Japanese	S		M		L		LL

In Japan, you specify length by using the metric system. If your waist is **30 inchi** (sahn-jooo-een chee;

30 inches), it's **76.2 senchi** (nah-nah-jooo-roh-koo tehn nee sehn-chee; 76.2 centimeters). To find your size in centimeters, multiply your size in inches by 2.54 (1 inch = 2.54 centimeters).

Words to Know

chōdo ii	chohh-doh eee	exact fit, just right
mijikai	mee-jee-kah-ee	short
nagai	nah-gah-ee	long
chīsai	cheee-sah-ee	small
ōkii	ohh-keee	big
saizu	sah-ee-zoo	size
shichakushitsu	shee-chah-koo-shee-tsoo	fitting room

Going to a Department Store

Depāto (deh-pahh-toh; department stores) are very convenient. Which departments interest you?

- **fujinfuku** (foo-jeen-foo-koo; women's clothes)
- **hōseki** (hohh-seh-kee; jewelry)
- **kaban** (kah-bahn; luggage)
- **kagu** (kah-goo; furniture)
- **keshōhin** (keh-shohh-heen; cosmetics)
- **kodomofuku** (koh-doh-moh-foo-koo; children's clothes)

- **kutsu** (koo-tsoo; shoes)

- **shinshifuku** (sheen-shee-foo-koo; men's clothes)

- **shoseki** (shoh-seh-kee; books)

- **supōtsu yōhin** (soo-pohh-tsoo yohh-heen; sporting goods)

Negotiating Prices

Kaimono (kah-ee-moh-noh; shopping) can be exciting. Visiting different **mise** (mee-seh; stores), checking out all the items, and comparing **nedan** (neh-dahn; prices) is my idea of a great afternoon.

Are you good at asking for **nebiki** (neh-bee-kee; discounts)? You can't just expect a discount — you have to be firm about asking for it. Here are a few phrases for talking about **nedan**:

- **Ikura desu ka.** (ee-koo-rah deh-soo kah; How much is it?)

- **Chotto takai desu.** (choht-toh tah-kah-ee deh-soo; It's a little expensive.)

- **Mō chotto yasuku shite kudasai.** (mohh choht-toh yah-soo-koo shee-teh koo-dah-sah-ee; Make it a bit cheaper please.)

- **Māmā yasui desu ne.** (mahh mahh yah-soo-ee deh-soo neh; It's relatively cheap.)

Conjugate the u-verb **kau** (to buy). Watch out for the *w* sound that appears in the negative form.

Form	Pronunciation
kau	kah-oo
kawanai	kah-wah-nah-ee
kai	kah-ee
katte	kaht-teh

Words to Know

kaimono	kah-ee-moh-noh	shopping
Ikura desu ka?	ee-koo-rah deh-soo kah	How much?
nebiki	neh-bee-kee	discount
takai	tah-kah-ee	expensive
yasui	yah-soo-ee	cheap

Paying for Your Purchases

If you're going shopping, you need a **kurejitto kado** (koo-reh-jeet-toh kahh-doh; credit card) or some **o-satsu** (oh-sah-tsoo; bills) and a few **kōka** (kohh-kah; coins). When you **harau** (hah-rah-oo; pay), don't forget your **o-tsuri** (oh-tsoo-ree; change).

Conjugate the u-verb **harau** (hah-rah-oo; to pay). Watch out for the *w* sound that shows up in the negative form.

Form	Pronunciation
harau	hah-rah-oo
harawanai	hah-rah-wah-nah-ee
harai	hah-rah-ee
haratte	har-raht-teh

Words to Know

o-tsuri	oh-tsoo-ree	change
ryōshūsho	ryohh-shooo-shoh	receipt

| shōhizei | shohh-hee-zehh | sales tax |
| subete | soo-beh-teh | everything |

Going Grocery Shopping

Restaurants are great, but if you want to save time or money, shop for food. If you go to a **sūpāmāketto** (sooo-pahh-mahh-keht-toh; supermarket), you can get most of the items you need in one trip, including:

- ✔ **aisukurīmu** (ah-ee-soo-koo-reee-moo; ice cream)
- ✔ **gyūnyū** (gyooo-nyooo; milk)
- ✔ **jūsu** (jooo-soo; juice)
- ✔ **o-kome** (oh-koh-meh; uncooked rice)
- ✔ **pan** (pahn; bread)
- ✔ **tamago** (tah-mah-goh; eggs)

Going to a butcher

You can find these **niku** (nee-koo; meats) at a **nikuya-san** (nee-koo-yah-sahn; meat store):

- ✔ **butaniku** (boo-tah-nee-koo; pork)
- ✔ **gyūniku** (gyooo-nee-koo; beef)
- ✔ **shichimenchō** (shee-chee-mehn-chohh; turkey)
- ✔ **toriniku** (toh-ree-nee-koo; chicken)
- ✔ **hamu** (hah-moo; ham)
- ✔ **sōsēji** (sohh-sehh-jee; sausage)

Buying vegetables and fruit

You can buy **yasai** (yah-seh-ee; vegetables) and **kuda-mono** (koo-dah-moh-noh; fruits) in supermarkets, but if you go to a farm stand or a **yaoya-san** (yah-oh-yah-sahn; produce store/greenmarket), you'll get the freshest produce. Include some of the following healthful items on your **shoppingu risuto** (shohp-peen-goo ree-soo-toh; shopping list):

- ✔ **jagaimo** (jah-gah-ee-moh; potatoes)
- ✔ **mikan** (mee-kahn; oranges)
- ✔ **ninjin** (neen-jeen; carrots)
- ✔ **pīman** (peee-mahn; green peppers)
- ✔ **remon** (reh-mohn; lemons)
- ✔ **retasu** (reh-tah-soo; lettuce)
- ✔ **ringo** (reen-goh; apples)
- ✔ **tamanegi** (tah-mah-neh-gee; onions)
- ✔ **ichigo** (ee-chee-goh; strawberries)

Buying fresh fish

The Japanese are big fish eaters. If you're a fish lover, too, a fish market is the place for you. Remember the names of your favorite fish when you make the trip:

- ✔ **maguro** (mah-goo-roh; tuna)
- ✔ **masu** (mah-soo; trout)
- ✔ **sake** (sah-keh; salmon)
- ✔ **tai** (tah-ee; red snapper)
- ✔ **tara** (tah-rah; cod)

Chapter 7

Making Leisure a Top Priority

. . . .

In This Chapter

▶ Brushing up on art and culture

▶ Making plans with friends

▶ Discussing your hobbies

▶ Playing sports

. . . .

*N*o matter how much you love your **shigoto** (shee-goh-toh; job), your life can't be entirely healthy if it consists only of work. Set some time aside for **rekuriēshon** (reh-koo-ree-ehh-shohn; recreation). Expanding your interests will make you an even more interesting and attractive person.

Using the Verb Suru (To Do)

The verb **suru** (soo-roo; to do) is the most frequently used verb in Japanese. You use **suru** when you want to talk about doing many different types of activities, including most of those discussed in this chapter.

To start with, conjugate the verb **suru** (soo-roo; to do). It's an irregular verb.

Form	Pronunciation
suru	soo-roo
shinai	shee-nah-ee
shi	shee
shite	shee-teh

Table 7-1 shows some of the many fun (and some not-so-fun) things you can do with **suru.**

Table 7-1	Suru Activities	
Japanese	**Pronunciation**	**Translation**
benkyō o suru	behn-kyohh oh soo-roo	to study
kaimono o suru	kah-ee-moh-noh oh soo-roo	to do the shopping
kankō o suru	kahn-kohh oh soo-roo	to go sightseeing
karate o suru	kah-rah-teh oh soo-roo	to do karate
ryōri o suru	ryohh-ree oh soo-roo	to cook
sentaku o suru	sehn-tah-koo oh soo-roo	to do laundry
shukudai o suru	shoo-koo-dah-ee oh soo-roo	to do homework
sōji o suru	sohh-jee oh soo-roo	to clean
tenisu o suru	teh-nee-soo oh soo-roo	to play tennis
toranpu o suru	toh-rahn-poo oh soo-roo	to play cards

Japanese	Pronunciation	Translation
yamanobori o suru	yah-mah-noh-boh-ree o soo-roo	to mountain climb
zangyō o suru	zahn-gyohh oh soo-roo	to work overtime

The Japanese have created many verbs by adding the verb **suru** to a foreign word, including my favorite: **rirakkusu suru** (ree-rahk-koo-soo soo-roo; to relax).

You form lots of Japanese verbs by putting a noun in front of **suru** and conjugating **suru**.

Exploring Fun Places

I bet your town is full of opportunities for fun. Read the **shinbun** (sheen-boon; newspaper), pick up a few **zasshi** (zahs-shee; magazines), or surf the **Intānetto** (een-tahh-neht-toh; Internet) to find out what's going on.

Visiting museums and galleries

Museums and galleries are great places to soak up culture. Here are some common museum-related words:

- ✔ **hakubutsukan** (hah-koo-boo-tsoo-kahn; museum)
- ✔ **bijutsukan** (bee-joo-tsoo-kahn; art museum)
- ✔ **garō** (gah-rohh; gallery)
- ✔ **gējutsuhin** (gehh-joo-tsoo-heen; work of art)

You may want to ask these questions in a museum or gallery:

- ✔ **Hakubutsukan wa nan-ji ni akimasu ka.** (hah-koo-boo-tsoo-kahn wah nahn-jee nee ah-kee-mah-soo kah; What time does the museum open?)

> ✔ **Nan-ji ni shimarimasu ka.** (nahn-jee nee shee-mah-ree-mah-soo kah; What time does it close?)

> ✔ **Nichiyōbi wa oyasumi desu ka.** (nee-chee-yohh-bee wah oh-yah-soo-mee deh-soo kah; Is it closed on Sundays?)

Conjugate the u-verbs **aku** (ah-koo; to open) and **shimaru** (shee-mah-roo; to close).

Form	Pronunciation
aku	ah-koo
akanai	ah-kah-nah-ee
aki	ah-kee
aite	ah-ee-teh

Form	Pronunciation
shimaru	shee-mah-roo
shimaranai	shee-mah-rah-nah-ee
shimari	shee-mah-ree
shimatte	shee-maht-teh

Going to the theater

Visiting **gekijō** (geh-kee-johh; theaters) really lets you feel the passion of the performers.

> ✔ **gekijō** (geh-kee-johh; theater)

> ✔ **o-shibai** (oh-shee-bah-ee; play)

> ✔ **eigakan** (ehh-gah-kahn; movie theater)

> ✔ **eiga** (ehh-gah; movie)

> ✔ **konsāto** (kohn-sahh-toh)

To see a movie or play, you have to buy a **chiketto** (chee-keht-toh; ticket). These phrases should cover your ticket-buying needs:

> ✔ **Sumimasen. Konban no o-shibai wa nan-ji kara desu ka.** (soo-mee-mah-sehn. kohn-bahn noh oh-shee-bah-ee wah nahn-jee kah-rah deh-soo kah; Excuse me. What time does today's play start?)

✔ **Mada ii seki wa arimasu ka.** (mah-dah eee seh-kee wah ah-ree-mah-soo kah; Do you still have good seats?)

✔ **Ichiman-en no seki o ni-mai onegaishimasu.** (ee-chee-mahn-ehn noh seh-kee oh nee-mah-ee oh-neh-gah-ee-shee-mah-soo; Two for the 10,000-yen seats, please.)

✔ **Otona futari onegaishimasu.** (oh-toh-nah foo-tah-ree oh-neh-gah-ee-shee-mah-soo; Two adults, please.)

✔ **Otona futari to kodomo hitori onegaishimasu.** (oh-toh-nah foo-tah-ree toh koh-doh-moh hee-toh-ree oh-neh-gah-ee-shee-mah-soo; Two adults and one child, please.)

✔ **Shinia hitori onegaishimasu.** (shee-nee-ah hee-toh-ree oh-neh-gah-ee-shee-mah-soo; One senior citizen, please).

Use the counter **-mai** (mah-ee) for counting tickets because tickets are flat. (See Chapter 3 for a discussion of counters.)

Words to Know

konban	kohn-bahn	tonight
chiketto	chee-keht-toh	ticket
otona	oh-toh-nah	adult
seki	seh-kee	seat

Going to bars and clubs

Where do you **nomu** (noh-moo; drink)? Having a drink at home is usually a lot cheaper than going to a bar, but sometimes going to these places for a drink in a festive or fancy atmosphere is fun:

✔ **bā** (bahh; bar)

✔ **izakaya** (ee-zah-kah-yah; casual Japanese-style bar)

✔ **naitokurabu** (nah-ee-toh-koo-rah-boo; nightclub)

O-sake (oh-sah-keh) refers to both Japanese rice wine and alcoholic beverages in general. Take a walk over to the bar and order your favorite **o-sake**:

✔ **atsukan** (ah-tsoo-kahn; hot Japanese rice wine)

✔ **bīru** (beee-roo; beer)

✔ **burandē** (boo-rahn-dehh; brandy)

✔ **chūhai** (chooo-hah-ee; **shōchū** and tonic)

✔ **hiya** (hee-yah; cold sake)

✔ **jin** (jeen; gin)

✔ **kakuteru** (kah-koo-teh-roo; cocktail)

✔ **mizuwari** (mee-zoo-wah-ree; whiskey and water)

✔ **onzarokku** (ohn-zah-rohk-koo; whiskey on the rocks)

✔ **ramushu** (rah-moo-shoo; rum)

✔ **shōchū** (shohh-chooo; a Japanese liquor)

✔ **sutorēto** (soo-toh-rehh-toh; whiskey straight)

✔ **uisukī** (oo-ee-soo-keee; whiskey)

✔ **wokka** (wohk-kah; vodka)

✔ **wain** (wah-een; wine)

At a bar, these phrases come in handy:

✔ **Nani nomu.** (nah-nee noh-moo; What will you drink?)

✔ **Kyō wa nani ga oishii.** (kyohh wah nah-nee gah oh-ee-sheee; What's good today?)

✔ **Jā, sore.** (jahh soh-reh; Then I'll have that.)

Singing like a star at a karaoke bar

Karaoke (kah-rah-oh-keh) started in Japan as a form of after-work entertainment. It was viewed as a great way of releasing the daily **sutoresu** (soo-toh-reh-soo; stress) related to **shigoto** (shee-goh-toh; work). Today, karaoke is a popular **shumi** (shoo-mee; hobby) with everyone — men and women, young and old.

If you go to Japan, visit a karaoke **bā** (bahh; bar) at least once. Check the index of **kyoku** (kyoh-koo; musical pieces) and ask for the song you want to **utau** (oo-tah-oo; sing). When it's your **ban** (bahn; turn), sing into the **maiku** (mah-ee-koo; microphone) as you watch the **kashi** (kah-shee; lyrics) scroll across the **gamen** (gah-mehn; monitor). Sing like a **sutā** (soo-tahh; star), even if you're **onchi** (ohn-chee; tone deaf).

Talking about Your Hobbies

If you get to know a Japanese person socially, he or she may ask you **Shumi wa** (shoo-mee wah; What's your hobby?). Having at least one **shumi** (hobby) that you can talk proudly about is good. Is your **shumi** athletic, artistic, or academic in nature? Do you do any of the following activities?

- ✔ **dokusho** (doh-koo-shoh; reading)
- ✔ **engei** (ehn-gehh; gardening)
- ✔ **ikebana** (ee-keh-bah-nah; flower arranging)
- ✔ **kitte no korekushon** (keet-teh noh koh-reh-koo-shohn; stamp collecting)
- ✔ **ryori** (ryohh-ree; cooking)
- ✔ **tsuri** (tsoo-ree; fishing)

Exploring Nature

If you're tired of working in front of your **konpyūtā** (kohn-pyooo-tahh; computer), take a trip to the **yama** (yah-mah; mountains) or the **umi** (oo-mee; sea). Your eyes need a change of pace, and the beautiful **kumo** (koo-moh; clouds), the tall **ki** (kee; trees), and a **yotto** (yoht-toh; sailboat) or two on the **suiheisen** (soo-ee-hehh-sehn; horizon) can provide a nice break.

While enjoying **shizen** (shee-zehn; nature), you may want to use a few of the words in Table 7-2.

Table 7-2	Nature Words	
Japanese	*Pronunciation*	*Translation*
bīchi	beee-chee	beach
kaigan	kah-ee-gahn	shoreline
kawa	kah-wah	river
kazan	kah-zahn	volcano
mizuumi	mee-zoo-oo-mee	lake
sabaku	sah-bah-koo	desert
sanmyaku	sahn-myah-koo	mountain range
sunahama	soo-nah-hah-mah	sandy beach
taki	tah-kee	waterfall
umi	oo-mee	sea/ocean
yama	yah-mah	mountain

In addition to admiring the scenery, you may want to go

- **haikingu** (hah-ee-keen-goo; hiking)
- **kyanpu** (kyahn-poo; camping)
- **saikuringu** (sah-ee-koo-reen-goo; cycling)
- **suiei** (soo-ee-ehh; swimming)

Living the Sporting Life

Do you participate in or watch **supotsu** (soo-pohh-tsoo; sports)? Whether you **suru** (soo-roo; play) or **miru** (mee-roo; watch), sports probably take up some of your time.

Yakyū (yah-kyooo; baseball) and **sakkā** (sahk-kahh; soccer) are the most popular sports in Japan, but people also enjoy other sports, such as

- **barēbōru** (bah-rehh-bohh-roo; volleyball)
- **basukettobōru** (bah-soo-keht-toh-bohh-roo; basketball)
- **futtoboru** (foot-toh-bohh-roo; football)
- **gorufu** (goh-roo-foo; golf)
- **sukēto** (soo-kehh-toh; skating)
- **sukī** (soo-keee; skiing)
- **sāfin** (sahh-feen; surfing)
- **tenisu** (teh-nee-soo; tennis)

Sumō (soo-mohh; sumo wrestling) is the national sport in Japan. The object of **sumō** is to push your opponent out of a ring or to force any part of his body, other than the soles of his feet, to touch the ground. Believe it or not, many strong **sumō** wrestlers are from America! If you're interested in becoming a **sumō** wrestler in Japan, start overeating and gain at least 300 pounds!

Saying "I Can"

To say that you "can" do something rather than that you "do" something, add a suffix (**-eru** or **-rareru**) to the verb. You need to do a little surgery to attach the suffix to the verb. Both the amount of surgery necessary and the suffix you add depend on the class of the verb.

✔ If the verb is a u-verb, remove the *u* at the end of the verb in the dictionary form and add **-eru**. For example, **aruku** (ah-roo-koo; to walk) is a u-verb. Removing the final *u* and adding **-eru** gives you **arukeru** (ah-roo-keh-roo). **Aruku** means "I walk," but **arukeru** means "I can walk."

✔ If the verb is a ru-verb, remove the **ru** at the end of the verb in the dictionary form and add **-rareru**. For example, the verb **okiru** (oh-kee-roo; to get up) is a ru-verb. Removing **ru** and adding **-rareru** gives you **okirareru** (oh-kee-rah-reh-roo), which means "I can get up."

The only necessary sound adjustment in this process is to change **ts** to **t** before adding **-eru**. So the "can" form of the verb **motsu** (moh-tsoo; to hold) is **moteru** (moh-teh-roo; can hold), not **motseru** (moh-tseh-roo). **Motsu** isn't an irregular verb — it's just that **tse** (tseh) isn't an authentic Japanese sound, so it gets simplified to **te** (teh).

And I should tell you what happens to two of the major irregular verbs, **suru** (soo-roo; to do) and **kuru** (koo-roo; to come), in the "can" situation. The "can" form of the verb **suru** is **dekiru** (deh-kee-roo; can do), and the "can" form of the verb **kuru** is **korareru** (koh-rah-reh-roo; can come).

When you use a "can" form in a sentence, replace the direct object particle **o** (oh) with the particle **ga** (gah). Even though it's not a subject, you have to mark it with the particle **ga** anyway. So **sushi o tsukuru** (soo-shee oh tsoo-koo-roo) means "you make sushi," but **sushi ga tsukureru** (soo-shee gah tsoo-koo-reh-roo) means "you can make sushi."

Now tell me what you can do and what your friends and family can do:

✔ **Watashi wa Nihongo ga hanasemasu.** (wah-tah-shee wah nee-hohn-goh gah hah-nah-seh-mah-soo; I can speak Japanese.)

✔ **Adamu wa karate ga dekimasu.** (ah-dah-moo wah kah-rah-teh gah deh-kee-mah-soo; Adam can do karate.)

✔ **Chichi wa Nihongo ga hanasemasen.** (chee-chee wah nee-hohn-goh gah han-nah-seh-mah-sehn; My father can't speak Japanese.)

✔ **Kurisu wa hashi ga tsukaemasu.** (koo-ree-soo wah hah-shee gah tsoo-kah-eh-mah-soo; Chris can use chopsticks.)

Using Your Artistic Talent

Don't be afraid to express your **kimochi** (kee-moh-chee; feelings) and **kangae** (kahn-gah-eh; ideas) artistically. Use your **sozoryoku** (sohh-zohh-ryoh-koo; creativity). You can even use the same techniques that you used as a **kodomo** (koh-doh-moh; child).

Which of the following art forms interests you?

✔ **chōkoku** (chohh-koh-koo; sculpting, engraving)

✔ **kaiga** (kah-ee-gah; painting, drawing)

✔ **kirutingu** (kee-roo-teen-goo; quilting)

✔ **togei** (tohh-gehh; pottery)

If you go to Japan, visit **karuchā sentā** (kah-roo-chahh sehn-tahh; cultural centers or cultural schools). You can observe classes in traditional Japanese arts like

✔ **ikebana** (ee-keh-bah-nah; flower arranging)

✔ **ryori** (ryohh-ree; cooking)

✔ **sado** (sah-dohh; tea ceremony)

✔ **shodo** (shoh-dohh; calligraphy)

Do you play a **gakki** (gahk-kee; musical instrument)? If you don't, try one of these **gakki:**

✔ **piano** (pee-ah-noh; piano)

✔ **baiorin** (bah-ee-oh-reen; violin)

- ✔ **doramu** (doh-rah-moo; drums)
- ✔ **furūto** (foo-rooo-toh; flute)
- ✔ **gitā** (gee-tahh; guitar)
- ✔ **erekigitā** (eh-reh-kee gee-tahh; electric guitar)
- ✔ **sakusofon** (sah-koo-soh-fohn; saxophone)
- ✔ **toranpetto** (toh-rahn-peht-toh; trumpet)

For different types of musical instruments, you use different verbs to mean "to play." For wind instruments, use the verb **fuku** (foo-koo). For a stringed instrument or a keyboard, use the verb **hiku** (hee-koo). Other instruments need specific verbs:

- ✔ **baiorin o hiku** (bah-ee-oh-reen oh hee-koo; to play the violin)
- ✔ **doramu o tataku** (doh-rah-moo oh tah-tah-koo; to play the drums)
- ✔ **furūto o fuku** (foo-rooo-toh oh foo-koo; to play the flute)
- ✔ **orugan o hiku** (oh-roo-gahn oh hee-koo; to play the organ)
- ✔ **piano o hiku** (pee-ah-noh oh hee-koo; to play the piano)
- ✔ **toranpetto o fuku** (toh-rahn-peht-toh oh foo-koo; to play the trumpet)

Words to Know

ressun	rehs-soon	lessons
happyokai	hahp-pyohh-kah-ee	recital
rokku bando	rohk-koo bahn-doh	rock band
renshū suru [irr]	rehn-shooo soo-roo	to practice

Giving and Receiving Invitations

Hanging out with friends is always fun. **Sasou** (sah-soh-oo; invite) your friends out for a night on the town or simply invite some people over to watch a movie. To start with, conjugate the u-verb **sasou** (sah-soh-oo; to invite):

Form	*Pronunciation*
sasou	sah-soh-oo
sasowanai	sah-soh-wah-nah-ee
sasoi	sah-soh-ee
sasotte	sah-soht-teh

Making a suggestion using "why don't we?"

If you want to go somewhere with your friend, make a suggestion by saying "Why don't we go there?"; "How about going there?"; or "Would you like to go there?" The easiest, most natural, and least pushy way of making a suggestion in Japanese is to ask a question that ends in **-masen ka** (mah-sehn kah). **-Masen ka** is the polite negative ending **-masen** plus the question particle **ka.**

Why negative? In English, you say things like "Why don't we go to the bar tonight?" That form is negative, too. Make sure that the verb before **-masen ka** is in the stem form, as in **Ikimasen ka** (ee-kee-mah-sehn kah; Why don't we go there?). The **iki** part is the stem form of the verb **iku** (ee-koo; to go). If you want to do something, use verbs like **suru** (soo-roo; to do) and **taberu** (tah-beh-roo; to eat).

- ✔ **Eigakan ni ikimasen ka.** (ehh-gah-kahn nee ee-kee-mah-sehn kah; Why don't we go to a movie theater tonight?)

- ✔ **Itsuka isshoni tenisu o shimasen ka.** (ee-tsoo-kah ees-shoh-nee teh-nee-soo oh shee-mah-sehn kah; Why don't we play tennis together someday?)

✔ **Kondo isshoni robusutā o tabemasen ka.** (kohn-doh ees-shoh-nee roh-boo-soo-tahh oh tah-beh-mah-sehn kah; How about eating lobster together next time?)

Saying "let's go" and "shall we go?"

In English, you can invite friends to an activity by saying "Let's go there" or "Let's do it." Saying "let's" in Japanese is easy: Get a verb in the stem form and add the ending **-mashō** (mah-shohh), as in **ikimashō** (ee-kee-mah-shohh; let's go) and **shimashō** (shee-mah-shohh; let's do it).

✔ **Isshoni utaimashō.** (ees-shoh-nee oo-tah-ee-mah-shohh; Let's sing together.)

✔ **Konban isshoni nomimashō.** (kohn-bahn ees-sho-nee noh-mee-mah-shohh; Let's drink together tonight.)

✔ **Kondo isshoni eiga o mimashō.** (kohn-doh ees-shoh-nee ehh-gah oh mee-mah-shohh; Let's see a movie together next time.)

To make a question using "Shall we," add **-mashō** to the end of the verb.

✔ **Chesu o shimashō ka.** (cheh-soo oh shee-mah-shohh kah; Shall we play chess?)

✔ **Kantorī Gāden ni ikimashō ka.** (kahn-toh-reee gahh-dehn nee ee-kee-mah-shohh kah; Shall we go to Country Garden?)

-Mashō ka also means "Shall I?" so you can use it to say something like "Shall I bring something?" or "Shall I help you?" The context usually clarifies whether **-mashō ka** means "Shall we?" or "Shall I?"

✔ **Nanika motteikimashō ka.** (nah-nee-kah moht-teh-ee-kee-mah-shohh kah; Shall I bring something?)

✔ **Tetsudaimashō ka.** (teh-tsoo-dah-ee-mah-shohh kah; Shall I help you?)

Inviting friends to your house

Clean up your house and buy some drinks and chips. Then you're ready to have some friends over! Use the verb **kuru** (koo-roo; to come) when you call. But before you invite anyone, practice conjugating the verb **kuru** (koo-roo; to come). It's an irregular verb.

Form	Pronunciation
kuru	koo-roo
konai	koh-nah-ee
ki	kee
kite	kee-teh

Here are some examples of the verb **kuru** in action:

- ✔ **Uchi ni kimasen ka.** (oo-chee nee kee-mah-sehn kah; Would you like to come to my house?)

- ✔ **Ashita watashi no apāto ni kimasen ka.** (ah-shee-tah wah-tah-shee noh ah-pahh-toh nee kee-mah-sehn kah; Would you like to come to my apartment tomorrow?)

If you're the one who gets invited, asking your friend what you can **motteiku** (moht-teh-ee-koo; bring) is a good idea. Japanese hosts tend to tell their guests not to bring anything, but bring something anyway.

Chapter 8

When You Gotta Work

- -

In This Chapter

▶ Talking business

▶ Managing yourself at the office

▶ Landing your dream job

▶ Using the telephone

- -

*L*ike it or not, most of us have to work. This chapter gives you the vocabulary you need to talk about your job, get around your office, and perform basic business tasks, such as making phone calls.

Talking about Your Job

To ask other people about their **shigoto** (shee-goh-toh; jobs), say **O-shigoto wa nan desu ka** (oh-shee-goh-toh wah nahn deh-soo kah; What's your job?). Or you can use the abbreviated version, **O-shigoto wa** (oh-shee-goh-toh wah; How about your job?).

Following are some occupations you or your conversational partner may hold:

> ✔ **bengoshi** (behn-goh-shee; lawyer)
>
> ✔ **isha** (ee-shah; medical doctor)
>
> ✔ **kangofu** (kahn-goh-foo; nurse)
>
> ✔ **jimuin** (jee-moo-een; secretary)
>
> ✔ **kameraman** (kah-meh-rah-mahn; photographer)

- **kenkyūin** (kehn-kyooo-een; researcher)
- **kokku** (kohk-koo; chef)
- **konpyūtā puroguramā** (kohn-pyooo-tahh poo-roh-goo-rah-mahh; computer programmer)
- **kyōju** (kyohh-joo; professor)
- **kyōshi** (kyohh-shee; teacher)
- **uētā** (oo-ehh-tahh; waiter)
- **uētoresu** (oo-ehh-toh-reh-soo; waitress)

If you just want to say that you work for a **kaisha** (kah-ee-shah; company) or that you're an office worker, you can use the term **kaishain** (kah-ee-shah-een; company employee). The Japanese typically identify themselves as **kaishain** without specifying their job titles or roles.

Managing Your Office Equipment

If you're a **seishain** (sehh-shah-een; full-time employee), you probably spend about one-third of your time at the **jimusho** (jee-moo-shoh; office). Why not make your **shokuba** (shoh-koo-bah; workplace) as comfortable as possible? While you're sitting in your **isu** (ee-soo; chair) at your **tsukue** (tsoo-koo-eh; desk), take a look around. What do you have on your desktop? What don't you have?

- **denwa** (dehn-wah; telephone)
- **fakusu** (fah-koo-soo; fax machine)
- **konpyūtā** (kohn-pyooo-tahh; computer)
- **kopīki** (koh-peee-kee; copier)
- **purintā** (poo-reen-tahh; printer)

Check inside your **hikidashi** (hee-kee-dah-shee; drawers) to see what office supplies you have:

- **bōrupen** (bohh-roo-pehn; ballpoint pen)
- **enpitsu** (ehn-pee-tsoo; pencil)

✔ **hochikisu** (hoh-chee-kee-soo; stapler)

✔ **keshigomu** (keh-shee-goh-moo; eraser)

✔ **noto** (nohh-toh; notebook)

✔ **serotēpu** (seh-roh-tehh-poo; tape)

If you can't find a pen or an eraser, ask a colleague. Use the verb **aru** (ah-roo; to exist) to ask "Do you have?" Add the polite suffix **-masu** (mah-soo) to the stem form of **aru,** as in **arimasu** (ah-ree-mah-soo), and make the phrase into a question by adding the question particle **ka** (kah), as in **arimasu ka** (ah-ree-mah-soo kah).

If you just ask **arimasu ka,** your colleague won't understand what you want. Mention the item you're asking about at the beginning of the sentence and place the topic particle **wa** (wah) right after the item you're inquiring about, as in these examples:

✔ **Hochikisu wa arimasu ka.** (hoh-chee-kee-soo wah ah-ree-mah-soo kah; Do you have a stapler?)

✔ **Keshigomu wa arimasu ka.** (keh-shee-goh-moo wah ah-ree-mah-soo kah; Do you have an eraser?)

Words to Know

jimusho	jee-moo-shoh	office
kaisha	kah-ee-shah	company
shigoto	shee-goh-toh	job
jōshi	johh-shee	boss
tsukue	tsoo-koo-eh	desk
dōryō	dohh-ryohh	co-worker

Searching for a Job

When you **sagasu** (sah-gah-soo; look for) a **shigoto** (shee-goh-toh; job), you need to get ready for the **mensetsu** (mehn-seh-tsoo; interview). Be prepared to talk about your **shokureki** (shoh-koo-reh-kee; work history) and your career goals.

Conjugate the verb **sagasu** (sah-gah-soo; to look for). **Sagasu** is a u-verb.

Form	Pronunciation
sagasu	sah-gah-soo
sagasanai	sah-gah-sah-nah-ee
sagashi	sah-gah-shee
sagashite	sah-gah-shee-teh

You may want to address the following issues:

- **kyūryō** (kyooo-ryohh; salary)
- **zangyō** (zahn-gyohh; overtime)
- **zangyō teate** (zahn-gyohh teh-ah-teh; overtime pay)
- **yūkyūkyūka** (yooo-kyooo-kyooo-kah; paid vacation)
- **kenkō hoken** (kehn-kohh hoh-kehn; health insurance)

When looking for a job, you want to know the duties and responsibilities associated with the position. For starters, you might ask these questions:

- **Watashi no shigoto wa nan desu ka.** (wah-tah-shee noh shee-goh-toh wah nahn deh-soo kah; What is my job?)
- **Sōji wa watashi no shigoto desu ka.** (sohh-jee wah wah-tah-shee noh shee-goh-toh deh-soo kah; Is cleaning my job?)

✔ **Doyōbi mo hatarakanakute wa ikemasen ka.**
(doh-yohh-bee mo hah-tah-rah-kah-nah-koo-teh wah ee-keh-mah-sehn kah; Do I have to work on Saturdays, too?)

Even after you start working in a new place, you have to figure out what to do each day. Conjugate the verb **hataraku** (hah-tah-rah-koo; to work). It's a u-verb.

Form	Pronunciation
hataraku	hah-tah-rah-koo
hatarakanai	hah-tah-rah-kah-nah-ee
hataraki	hah-tah-rah-kee
hataraite	hah-tah-rah-ee-teh

When you need to say "I have to" or "I must," use the verb in the negative form (see Chapter 2 for more on verb forms). Drop the final *i* (ee) and add **-kute wa ikemasen** (koo-teh wah ee-keh-mah-sehn) or **-kutewa ikenai** (koo-teh wah ee-keh-nah-ee). For example, the negative form of **taberu** (tah-beh-roo) is **tabenai** (tah-beh-nah-ee). By dropping the *i* and adding **-kute wa ikemasen,** you get **tabenakute wa ikemasen** (tah-beh-nah-koo-teh wah ee-keh-mah-sehn), which means "I have to eat." It's a mouthful, but it's the easiest way to express "have to" or "must" in Japanese. Take a look at these examples:

✔ **Ii shigoto o sagasanakute wa ikemasen.** (eee shee-goh-toh oh sah-gah-sah-nah-koo-teh wah ee-keh-mah-sehn; I have to look for a good job.)

✔ **Kyō wa zangyō o shinakute wa ikenai-n-desu.** (kyohh wa zahn-gyohh oh shee-nah-koo-teh wah ee-keh-nah-een-deh-soo; I have to work overtime today.)

Addressing your boss appropriately

Japan is very modern, but a shadow of feudalism still falls on the **shokuba** (shoh-koo-bah; workplace). **Buka** (boo-kah; subordinates) never address their **jōshi** (johh-shee; superiors) by their first names. If you work in Japan, address your **jōshi** by their titles and last names. If your **jōshi** is the **shachō** (shah-chohh; company president) and his last name is Smith, call him **Sumisu-shachō**. Address your **buka** by their last names, plus **-san** or **-kun**.

In a business context, both **-san** (sahn) and **-kun** (koon) can be used for women and men. So if Mr. Smith is your assistant, call him **Sumisu-san** (soo-mee-soo-sahn) or **Sumisu-kun** (soo-mee-soo-koon).

Here are some of the titles that Japanese companies use:

- ✔ **shachō** (shah-chohh; company president)
- ✔ **fukushachō** (foo-koo-shah-chohh; company vice president)
- ✔ **buchō** (boo-chohh; department chief)
- ✔ **kachō** (kah-chohh; section chief)
- ✔ **kakarichō** (kah-kah-ree-chohh; subsection chief)

Talking on the Phone

Denwa (dehn-wah; telephones) are an indispensable part of daily life. **Denshi mēru** (dehn-shee mehh-roo; e-mail) is great, too, but it can't replace the connection you get from hearing someone's **koe** (koh-eh; voice). This section gives you the essential phrases you need to have **denwa no kaiwa** (dehn-wah noh kah-ee-wah; telephone conversations) in Japanese.

Before you get ready to make a call in Japanese, get used to the Japanese words and terms related to telephone equipment, systems, and accessories:

✔ **denwa o kakeru** (dehn-wah oh kah-keh-roo; to make a phone call)

✔ **denwa o morau** (dehn-wah oh moh-rah-oo; to receive a phone call)

✔ **denwa-bangō** (dehn-wah-bahn-gohh; phone number)

✔ **denwachō** (dehn-wah-chohh; phone book)

✔ **kētai-denwa** (kehh-tah-ee-dehn-wah; cellular phone)

✔ **kōshū-denwa** (kohh-shooo-dehn-wah; public phone)

✔ **terefon-kādo** (teh-reh-fohn-kahh-doh; phone card)

Conjugate the verb **kakeru** (kah-keh-roo). You can use it in the phrase **denwa o kakeru** (dehn-wah oh kah-keh-roo; to make a phone call). It's a ru-verb.

Form	Pronunciation
kakeru	kah-keh-roo
kakenai	kah-keh-nah-ee
kake	kah-keh
kakete	kah-keh-teh

Calling a friend

Moshimoshi (moh-shee-moh-shee) in Japanese is a kind of line-testing phrase like "Hello, are you there?" or "Can you hear me?" Before you start talking, say **moshimoshi.**

Do you need to call your **tomodachi** (toh-moh-dah-chee; friend) to **hanasu** (hah-nah-soo; talk) about the **shukudai** (shoo-koo-dah-ee; homework) you haven't done yet? Or maybe you want to call your **tomodachi** just to **oshaberi o suru** (oh-sha-beh-ree oh soo-roo; chat).

If you call your friend's home and someone other than your friend picks up — her **okāsan** (oh-kahh-sahn; mom), for example — say your name before asking for your friend. If your name were Suzuki and you were calling your friend Ken, you'd say **Suzuki desu ga** (soo-zoo-kee deh-soo gah; This is Mr./Ms. Suzuki speaking) and then **Ken-san o onegaishimasu** (kehn-sahn oh oh-neh-gah-ee-shee-mah-soo; May I talk to Ken please?). If you don't tell her your name, she'll say **Dochira-sama desu ka** (doh-chee-rah-sah-mah deh-soo kah; Who is calling please?).

Words to Know

moshimoshi	moh-shee-moh-shee	Hello, are you there?
hanasu [u]	hah-nah-soo	talk
oshaberi o suru [irr]	oh-sha-beh-ree oh soo-roo	chat
_____-san o onegaishimasu.	-sahn oh oh-neh-gah-ee-shee-mah-soo	May I talk to Mr./Ms. _____ please?
Chotto matte kudasai.	choht-toh maht-teh koo-dah-sah-ee	Hold on please.
Dochira-sama desu ka.	doh-chee-rah-sah-mah deh-soo kah	Who's calling?

Calling hotels and stores

When you call commercial institutions such as **hoteru** (hoh-teh-roo; hotels), **mise** (mee-seh; stores), and

resutoran (reh-soo-toh-rahn; restaurants), the employ-
ees introduce the business first by saying **de gozaimasu** (deh goh-zah-ee-mah-soo) — the super-polite
version of the verb **desu** (deh-soo; to be). Of course,
with Japanese sentence construction, you'll hear the
name of the business before **de gozaimasu.** For example, **Hoteru Sanraizu de gozaimasu** (hoh-teh-roo sahn-
rah-ee-zoo deh goh-zah-ee-ma-soo) means "This is
Hotel Sunrise."

After an employee answers the phone, tell him or her
whom you want to speak to:

- ✔ **Adamu Jonson-san o onegaishimasu.** (ah-dah-
  moo john-sohn-sahn oh oh-neh-gah-ee-shee-mah-
  soo; May I speak to Mr. Adam Johnson please?)

- ✔ **Naisen 403-ban ni tsunaide kudasai.** (nah-ee-
  sehn yohn-hyah-koo-sahn-bahn nee tsoo-nah-
  ee-deh koo-dah-sah-ee; Please connect me to
  extension 403.)

- ✔ **Eigyōbu no kata o onegaishimasu.** (ehh-gyohh-
  boo noh kah-tah oh oh-neh-gah-ee-shee-mah-
  soo; I'd like to speak to someone in the sales
  department.)

When you call a commercial institution, you may be
put on hold for several minutes. Check out these
phrases for "waiting":

- ✔ **Mō 30-pun matte iru-n-desu ga.** (mohh sahn-
  joop-poon maht-teh ee-roon-deh-soo gah; I've
  been waiting for 30 minutes.)

- ✔ **O-matase shimashita.** (oh-mah-tah-seh shee-
  mah-shee-tah; Sorry to have kept you waiting.)

- ✔ **Shōshō o-machi kudasai.** (shohh shohh oh-mah-
  chee koo-dah-sah-ee; Could you wait a little
  please?)

Asking for what you want

Why do you make a phone call? Because you want to
talk to someone. Why do you want to talk to someone?

Maybe you want to tell him or her what you want. But how do you say "to want" in Japanese?

Although the Japanese do want things, there's no Japanese verb that means "to want." But fear not: Japanese has an adjective that means "to want." Actually, the Japanese use different adjectives to express "to want" depending on whether they want to perform an action or want some item.

Do you want to **kau** (kah-oo; buy) a big house with a tennis court and a swimming pool? Do you want to **taberu** (tah-beh-roo; eat) as much as you want without worrying about your health or your weight? Or do you want to **iku** (ee-koo; go) to Japan? Saying the phrases *to want to buy, to want to eat,* and *to want to go* in Japanese is easy. Simply add the suffix **-tai** (tah-ee) to the end of the stem form of the verb, as in **kaitai** (kah-ee-tah-ee; to want to buy), **tabetai** (tah-beh-tah-ee; to want to eat), and **ikitai** (ee-kee-tah-ee; to want to go). Use these **-tai** phrases just like you use regular i-type adjectives (Chapter 2 has more on these adjectives). Check out these examples:

- ✔ **Watashi wa yasumitai desu.** (wah-tah-shee wah yah-soo-mee-tah-ee deh-soo; I want to rest.)

- ✔ **Watashi wa atarashii kuruma o kaitai desu.** (wah-tah-shee wah ah-tah-rah-sheee koo-roo-mah oh kah-ee-tah-ee deh-soo; I want to buy a new car.)

- ✔ **Hawai ni ikitai desu.** (hah-wah-ee nee ee-kee-tah-ee deh-soo; I want to go to Hawaii.)

- ✔ **Nani o shitai desu ka.** (nah-nee oh shee-tah-ee deh-soo kah; What do you want to do?)

- ✔ **Uchi ni kaeritai desu.** (oo-chee nee kah-eh-ree-tah-ee deh-soo; I want to return home.)

When you call a store, restaurant, or hotel to tell them what you want — or when you tell anyone what you want — end your statement with **-n-desu ga** (n-deh-soo gah). This phrase injects a friendly, cooperative tone.

The function of **-n-desu** is to show your willingness to hear the other person's response; the **ga** is actually the sentence-ending particle that means "but." You're literally saying "I want to do such and such, but." What you actually mean is something like "I want to do such and such, but is it okay with you?"

Suppose you call a hotel to make a **yoyaku** (yoh-yah-koo; reservation). If you say **yoyaku o shitai desu** (yoh-yah-koo oh shee-tah-ee deh-soo), it means "I want to make a reservation." But phrasing your statement this way sounds too blunt in Japanese — you almost sound like you're making a protest or stating a demand. By contrast, if you say **yoyaku o shitai-n-desu ga** (yoh-yah-koo oh shee-tah-een-deh-soo gah), it means something like "I'd like to make a reservation, but could you help me with it?" Now your statement sounds soft, and you're kindly inviting the clerk's reply.

Calling a client

If you're a businessperson, you probably call your **shigoto no o-kyaku-san** (shee-goh-toh noh oh-kyah-koo-sahn; clients) constantly. And you probably know the important role phone conversations play in maintaining good relationships. You don't want to sound pushy or arrogant, but you don't want to sound unsophisticated or unintelligent, either.

When you call your **shigoto no o-kyaku-san** (shee-goh-toh noh oh-kyah-koo-sahn; clients), remember that you represent your **kaisha** (kah-ee-shah; company) or **mise** (mee-seh; store). Mention the name of your **kaisha** or **mise** first, before your own name. Instead of saying "This is Mr. White," for example, say "This is ABC Technology's Mr. White."

Greet your **o-kyaku-san** (oh-kyah-koo-sahn; client) and his or her **hisho** (hee-shoh; secretary) with **O-sewa ni natte orimasu** (oh-seh-wah nee naht-teh oh-ree-mah-soo; Thank you for doing business with us). It's one of the essential set phrases in Japanese business.

Words to Know		
hisho	hee-shoh	secretary
mise	mee-seh	store
o-kyaku-san	oh-kyah-koo-sahn	customer/ client
O-sewa ni natteorimasu.	oh-seh-wah nee naht-teh oh-ree-mah-soo	Thank you for doing business with us.

Leaving a message

Talking to someone voice-to-voice is difficult nowadays. We often communicate by leaving **dengon** (dehn-gohn; messages) for each other while our **isogashii seikatsu** (ee-soh-gah-sheee sehh-kah-tsoo; busy lives) keep going. You may leave a message on a **rusuban-denwa** (roo-soo-bahn-dehn-wah; answering machine) or with **dareka** (dah-reh-kah; someone).

What do you do with a **dengon** (dehn-gohn; message)? You **nokosu** (noh-koh-soo; leave) it. So conjugate the u-verb **nokosu**. Remember, it means "to leave" in the sense of leaving a message but not "to leave" in the sense of departing.

Form	Pronunciation
nokosu	noh-koh-soo
nokosanai	noh-koh-sah-nah-ee
nokoshi	noh-koh-shee
nokoshite	noh-koh-shee-teh

A message between friends might sound like the following:

Moshimoshi. Yukiko-san. Arekkusu desu. Ashita isshoni eiga o mimasen ka. Yokattara o-denwa o kudasai. 03-3355-5532 desu. Dōmo.

moh-shee-moh-shee. yoo-kee-koh-sahn. ah-rehk-koo-soo deh-soo. ah-shee-tah ees-shoh-nee ehh-gah oh mee-mah-sehn kah. yoh-kaht-tah-rah oh-dehn-wah oh koo-dah-sah-ee. zeh-roh-sahn sahn-sahn-goh-goh goh-goh-sahn-nee deh-soo. dohh-moh.

Hello Yukiko. This is Alex. Would you like to see a movie with me tomorrow? Please call me at 03-3355-5532, if it's okay with you. Thanks.

When you leave a message on an answering machine, clarify which person will call the other back:

- ✔ **Kaettara denwa o kudasai.** (kah-eht-tah-rah dehn-wah oh koo-dah-sah-ee; When you get back, please give me a call.)

- ✔ **Mata denwa o shimasu.** (mah-tah dehn-wah oh shee-mah-soo; I'll call you again.)

- ✔ **Yokattara o-denwa o kudasai.** (yoh-kaht-tah-rah oh-dehn-wah oh koo-dah-sah-ee; If you don't mind, could you give me a call?)

When you leave a message with a person, be clear about what you want. If you're leaving a message for a business contact, use these polite phrases:

- ✔ **Denwa ga atta koto o o-tsutae kudasai.** (dehn-wah gah aht-tah koh-toh oh oh-tsoo-tah-eh koo-dah-sah-ee; Please tell him/her that I called.)

- ✔ **Mata kochira kara o-denwa o itashimasu.** (mah-tah koh-chee-rah kah-rah oh-dehn-wah oh ee-tah-shee-mah-soo; I will call him/her again.)

- ✔ **O-denwa o itadakitai-n-desu ga.** (oh-dehn-wah oh ee-tah-dah-kee-tah-een-deh-soo gah; Would you kindly ask him/her to please call me back?)

The particle **to,** as in **to tsutaete kudasai** (toh tsoo-tah-eh-teh koo-dah-sah-ee; please tell so-and-so), is a quotation particle. Place it right after your message to indicate what your message is. Use it with verbs like **iu** (ee-oo; to say), **kaku** (kah-koo; to write), and **tsu-taeru** (tsoo-tah-eh-roo; to report/tell), as in the following examples:

- **10,000-en karita to kakimashita.** (ee-chee-mahn-ehn kah-ree-tah toh kah-kee-mah-shee-tah; I wrote that I borrowed 10,000 yen.)

- **Tanaka-san wa kuru to īmashita.** (tah-nah-kah-sahn wah koo-roo toh eee-mah-shee-tah; Mr. Tanaka said that he will come.)

- **Mata kimasu to tsutaete kudasai.** (mah-tah kee-mah-soo toh tsoo-tah-eh-teh koo-dah-sah-ee; Could you tell him/her that I'll come again?)

Go- (goh) is another polite prefix, just like **o-** (oh) (see Chapter 3). You can add **go-** to the beginning of a noun to refer respectfully to other people's items. Whether you use **go-** or **o-** depends on the noun — you just have to memorize which prefix goes with which nouns. Check out some examples:

- **go-dengon** (goh-dehn-gohn; message)

- **go-shōtai** (goh-shohh-tah-ee; invitation)

- **o-denwa** (oh-dehn-wah; telephone)

Chapter 9

I Get Around: Transportation

Kōtsū kikan (kohh-tsooo kee-kahn; transportation) is an indispensable part of life. This chapter provides you with essential phrases for getting around town.

Getting Around at the Airport

Taking a **hikōki** (hee-kohh-kee; airplane) is often necessary for business and leisure trips. If you take a **kokusaibin** (koh-koo-sah-ee-been; international flight), don't forget to bring your **pasupōto** (pah-soo-pohh-toh; passport). You also may need a **biza** (bee-zah; visa) depending on where you're coming from, where you're going, and the purpose and duration of your visit.

Getting on board

Table 9-1 lists some useful terms that relate to checking in at the airport and boarding your plane.

Table 9-1	Airport Vocabulary	
Japanese	*Pronunciation*	*Translation*
kūkō	kooo-kohh	airport
seki	seh-kee	seat
bin	been	flight
mado gawa no seki	mah-doh gah-wah noh seh-kee	window seat
tsūro gawa no seki	tsooo-roh gah-wah noh seh-kee	aisle seat
tōjō tetsuzuki	tohh-johh teh-tsoo-zoo-kee	check-in
menzeiten	mehn-zehh-tehn	duty-free shops
gēto	gehh-toh	gate
shukkoku tetsuzuki	shook-koh-koo teh-tsoo-zoo-kee	departure immigration

To specify a flight number, add **-bin** (been; flight), right after the number. For example, **18-bin** (jooo-hah-chee-been) means Flight 18. **Bin** means "flight" and also functions as a counter that specifies which flight.

The verb **noru** (noh-roo), a u-verb, is used for all forms of transportation, so its translation can be "to ride," "to get on," or "to get in." Pay close attention to the *r* syllables as you conjugate it.

Form	*Pronunciation*
noru	noh-roo
noranai	noh-rah-nah-ee
nori	noh-ree
notte	noht-teh

Remember to mark the form of transportation you're taking with the particle **ni** (nee), as in these examples:

✔ **hikōki ni noru** (hee-kohh-kee nee noh-roo; to get on an airplane)

✔ **jitensha ni noru** (jee-tehn-shah nee noh-roo; to ride a bike)

✔ **densha ni noru** (dehn-shah nee noh-roo; to get on a train)

✔ **takushī ni noru** (tah-koo-sheee nee noh-roo; to get in a taxi)

On the plane, ask the **suchuwādo** (soo-choo-wahh-doh; male flight attendant) or **suchuwādesu** (soo-choo-wahh-deh-soo; female flight attendant) any questions you may have, such as

✔ **Eiga wa nan-ji kara desu ka.** (ehh-gah wah nahn-jee kah-rah deh-soo kah; What time does the movie start?)

✔ **Nan-ban gēto ni tsukimasu ka.** (nahn-bahn gehh-toh nee tsoo-kee-mah-soo kah; Which gate are we arriving at?)

✔ **Nan-ji ni tsukimasu ka.** (nahn-jee nee tsoo-kee-mah-soo kah; What time will we arrive?)

Unless you want to live on an airplane, you also need to know the verb **oriru** (oh-ree-roo; to get off). You can use **oriru** for any form of transportation. Here are a couple of airport-related examples:

✔ **Hikōki kara orimashita.** (hee-kohh-kee kah-rah oh-ree-mah-shee-tah; I got off the airplane.)

✔ **Ushiro no deguchi kara orite kudasai.** (oo-shee-roh noh deh-goo-chee kah-rah oh-ree-teh koo-dah-sah-ee; Please get off via the rear exit.)

Here's how you conjugate the ru-verb **oriru**:

Form	Pronunciation
oriru	oh-ree-roo
orinai	oh-ree-nah-ee
ori	oh-ree
orite	oh-ree-teh

Going through immigration

Before entering a foreign country, you have to meet the folks in **nyūkoku shinsa** (nyooo-koh-koo sheen-sah; immigration) and **zeikan** (zehh-kahn; customs). If you're arriving in Japan, go to the **gaikokujin** (gah-ee-koh-koo-jeen; foreigner) booth and be ready for these questions and requests:

- ✔ **Pasupotō o misete kudasai.** (pah-soo-pohh-toh oh mee-seh-teh koo-dah-sah-ee; Show me your passport, please.)
- ✔ **Biza wa.** (bee-zah wah; How about your visa?)
- ✔ **Dono bin de kimashita ka.** (doh-noh been deh kee-mah-shee-tah kah; Which flight did you take to come here?)
- ✔ **Kankō desu ka.** (kahn-kohh deh-soo kah; Are you here for sightseeing?)
- ✔ **Shigoto desu ka.** (shee-goh-toh deh-soo kah; Are you here for business?)
- ✔ **Doko ni tomarimasu ka.** (doh-koh nee toh-mah-ree-mah-soo kah; Where are you staying?)

Words to Know

nyūkoku shinsa	nyooo-koh-koo sheen-sah	immigration
pasupotō	pah-soo-pohh-toh	passport
biza	bee-zah	visa

Going through customs

After you get through immigration, go to **tenimotsu hikiwatashijō** (teh-nee-moh-tsoo hee-kee-wah-tah-shee-johh; baggage claim) and pick up your bags. Then proceed to **zeikan** (zehh-kahn; customs) and pay the **zeikin** (zehh-keen; tax), if necessary. Certain items are **menzei** (mehn-zehh; duty-free) only if you bring less than a certain quantity. Familiarize yourself with the following questions and phrases:

- ✔ **Shinkoku suru mono wa arimasen ka.** (sheen-koh-koo soo-roo moh-noh wah ah-ree-mah-sehn kah; Is there anything you want to declare?)

- ✔ **Sūtsukesu o akete kudasai.** (sooo-tsoo-kehh-soo oh ah-keh-teh koo-dah-sah-ee; Open your suitcase, please.)

- ✔ **Minomawari no mono desu.** (mee-noh-mah-wah-ree noh moh-noh deh-soo; They are my personal belongings.)

- ✔ **Asoko de zeikin o haratte kudasai.** (ah-soh-koh deh zehh-keen oh hah-raht-teh koo-dah-sah-ee; Pay the tax over there, please.)

Conjugate the ru-verb **akeru** (ah-keh-roo; to open).

Form	Pronunciation
akeru	ah-keh-roo
akenai	ah-keh-nah-ee
ake	ah-keh
akete	ah-keh-teh

Getting Around Town

Which form of **kōtsū kikan** (kohh-tsooo kee-kahn; transportation) you take depends on where you are and where you want to go. Table 9-2 lists several forms of transportation.

Table 9-2	Modes of Transportation	
Japanese	*Pronunciation*	*Translation*
basu	bah-soo	bus
baiku	bah-ee-koo	motorcycle

(continued)

Table 9-2 (continued)

Japanese	Pronunciation	Translation
chikatetsu	chee-kah-teh-tsoo	subway
densha	dehn-shah	train
fune	foo-neh	ship
jitensha	jee-tehn-shah	bicycle
kuruma	koo-roo-mah	car
rentakā	rehn-tah-kahh	rental car
takushī	tah-koo-sheee	taxi

Asking about the best

To ask questions like "Which transportation method is cheapest?" and "Can you tell me the best way to get there?" use the question word **dono** (doh-noh; which) or **dore** (doh-reh; which one). If you're asking *which* of a particular thing, use **dono** and add the thing you're asking about right after it, as in these examples:

> ✔ **Dono basu ni norimasu ka.** (doh-noh bah-soo nee noh-ree-mah-soo kah; Which bus are you getting on?)

> ✔ **Dono densha de ikimasu ka.** (doh-noh dehn-shah deh ee-kee-mah-soo kah; By which train are you going there?)

If what you're asking about is understood in the context or has already been stated, you don't have to repeat the word. Just use **dore** (which one):

> ✔ **Dore ni norimasu ka.** (doh-reh nee noh-ree-mah-soo kah; Which one are you getting on?)

> ✔ **Dore de ikimasu ka.** (doh-reh deh ee-kee-mah-soo kah; By which one are you going there?)

Next, you have to form a question by inserting the key ingredient for *most/-est* — the adverb **ichiban** (ee-chee-bahn; the most/-est). In this case, **ichiban** comes before the adjective. If you recognize the word **ichiban** as the Japanese word for "first," you're right. It literally means "number one." Check out these examples:

- ✔ **Dono basu ga ichiban hayai desu ka.** (doh-noh bah-soo gah ee-chee-bahn hah-yah-ee deh-soo kah; Which bus is the fastest?)

- ✔ **Dore ga ichiban yasui desu ka.** (doh-reh gah ee-chee-bahn yah-soo-ee deh-soo kah; Which one is the cheapest?)

If you want to alert listeners that they must choose from the list you provide, you can list the items at the beginning of the question. Just place the particle **to** (toh) at the end of each item, as in

- ✔ **Takushī to, densha to, basu to, dore ga ichi-ban hayai desu ka.** (tah-koo-sheee toh, dehn-shah toh, bah-soo toh, doh-reh gah ee-chee-bahn hah-yah-ee deh-soo kah; Which is the fastest, taxis, trains, or buses?)

- ✔ **Hikōki to, kuruma to, densha to, basu to, dore ga ichi-ban anzen desu ka.** (hee-kohh-kee toh, koo-roo-mah toh, dehn-shah toh, bah-soo toh, doh-reh gah ee-chee-bahn ahn-zehn deh-soo kah; Which is the safest, airplanes, cars, trains, or buses?)

If you're comparing people, use **dare** (dah-reh; who) instead of **dore.** If you're comparing locations, use **doko** (doh-koh; where). To ask a question that compares two items, use **dochira** (doh-chee-rah; which one of the two), regardless of what the two items are.

Getting on a bus

Basu (bah-soo; buses) are inexpensive and convenient, and they can take you across town or across the country. Here are some useful bus-related terms:

- **basu tāminaru** (bah-soo tahh-mee-nah-roo; bus terminal)

- **basutē** (bah-soo-tehh; bus stop)

- **unchin** (oon-cheen; fare)

- **norikae** (noh-ree-kah-eh; transfer)

Hopping on a train

Traveling by **densha** (dehn-shah; train) is fun. You go through many **eki** (eh-kee; train stations), which represent the people who live or work in those towns.

First, check the direction of your train:

- **kudari densha** (koo-dah-ree dehn-shah; down train, traveling away from Tokyo)

- **nobori densha** (noh-boh-ree dehn-shah; up train, traveling toward Tokyo)

- **ōsaka yuki** (ohh-sah-kah yoo-kee; bound for Osaka)

- **Tōkyō hatsu Nagoya yuki** (tohh-kyohh hah-tsoo nah-goh-yah yoo-kee; departing from Tokyo and bound for Nagoya)

Choose from one of these types of trains, listed in descending order of speed and distance:

- **shinkansen** (sheen-kahn-sehn; bullet train)

- **tokkyū** (tohk-kyooo; super-express)

- **kaisoku** (kah-ee-soh-koo; rapid)

- **kyūkō** (kyooo-kohh; express)

- **futsū** (foo-tsooo; local)

When you take a train, make sure you know what time it **deru** (deh-roo; leaves) and **tsuku** (tsoo-koo; arrives). Conjugate the ru-verb **deru** (deh-roo; to leave) and the u-verb **tsuku** (tsoo-koo; to arrive).

Form	Pronunciation
deru	deh-roo
denai	deh-nah-ee
de	deh
dete	deh-teh

Form	Pronunciation
tsuku	tsoo-koo
tsukanai	tsoo-kah-nah-ee
tsuki	tsoo-kee
tsuite	tsoo-ee-teh

Table 9-3 provides a handy list of train-related vocabulary.

Table 9-3	Train-Related Terms	
Japanese	*Pronunciation*	*Translation*
jikokuhyō	jee-koh-koo-hyohh	timetable
hatsu	hah-tsoo	departure
chaku	chah-koo	arrival
hōmu	hohh-moo	platform
unchin	oon-cheen	fare
kippu	keep-poo	tickets
ōfuku	ohh-foo-koo	round-trip
katamichi	kah-tah-mee-chee	one-way
otona	oh-toh-nah	adult
kodomo	koh-doh-moh	child
otoshiyori	oh-toh-shee-yoh-ree	senior
shintaishōgaisha	sheen-tah-ee shohh-gah-ee-shah	handicapped person

Hatsu and **chaku** are short forms of **hassha suru** (hahs-shah soo-roo; to depart) and **tōchaku suru** (tohh-chah-koo soo-roo; to arrive). Take a look at a few examples:

✓ **16-ji 15-fun hatsu** (jooo-roh-koo-jee jooo-goh-foon hah-tsoo; 16:15, or 4:15 p.m., departure)

✓ **20-ji 57-fun chaku** (nee-jooo-jee goh-jooo-nah-nah-foon chah-koo; 20:57, or 8:57 p.m., arrival)

✓ **7-ji 5-fun Tōkyō hatsu 10-ji 7-fun Osaka chaku** (shee-chee-jee goh-foon tohh-kyohh hah-tsoo jooo-jee nah-nah-foon ohh-sah-kah chah-koo; 7:05 a.m. Tokyo departure, 10:07 a.m. Osaka arrival)

Use the counter **-mai** to express the number of tickets you want to purchase. (See Chapter 2 for information on counters.) If you're taking the **shinkansen** (sheen-kahn-sehn; bullet train) or another **tokkyū densha** (tohk-kyoo dehn-shah; super-express train) in Japan, you'll need to buy two tickets: a **tokkyūken** (tohk-kyoo-kehn; super-express ticket) plus the regular **jōshaken** (johh-shah-kehn; passenger ticket). You may make a request like the following:

✓ **Nagoya made otona san-mai ōfuku onegaishimasu.** (nah-goh-yah mah-deh oh-toh-nah sahn-mah-ee ohh-foo-koo oh-neh-gah-ee-shee-mah-soo; To Nagoya, three round-trip tickets for adults, please.)

✓ **Ōsaka made otona ichi-mai to kodomo ni-mai onegaishimasu.** (ohh-sah-kah mah-deh oh-toh-nah ee-chee-mah-ee toh koh-doh-moh nee-mah-ee oh-neh-gah-ee-shee-mah-soo; To Osaka, one ticket for an adult and two tickets for children, please.)

✓ **Tōkyō made katamichi ichi-mai.** (tohh-kyohh mah-deh kah-tah-mee-chee ee-chee-mah-ee; To Tokyo, one one-way ticket, please.)

✓ **Tōkyō made no jōshaken to tokkyūken o kudasai.** (tohh-kyohh mah-deh noh johh-shah-kehn toh tohk-kyooo-kehn oh koo-dah-sah-ee; A passenger ticket and a super-express ticket to Tokyo, please.)

Find out which **hōmu** (hohh-moo; platform) your train is leaving from and say the number with the counter **-ban-sen** (bahn-sehn), such as **ichi-ban-sen** (ee-chee-bahn-sehn; track 1), **ni-ban-sen** (nee-bahn-sehn; track 2), and **san-ban-sen** (sahn-bahn-sehn; track 3).

Hailing a taxi

Takushī (tah-koo-sheee; taxis) come to where you are, so there's no need to walk. Unlike trains, you don't have to figure out which one you should take. And unlike buses, you don't need to wait for them. If you have three or four people in your group, taking a **takushī** may be cheaper than taking a train or a bus. Here are some phrases you may say or hear in a taxi:

- ✔ **Dochira made.** (doh-chee-rah mah-deh; To where?)

- ✔ **Kūkō made ikura gurai kakarimasu ka.** (kooo-kohh mah-deh ee-koo-rah goo-rah-ee kah-kah-ree-mah-soo kah; How much does it cost to the airport?)

- ✔ **Bijutsukan made onegai shimasu.** (beé-joo-tsoo-kahn mah-deh oh-neh-gah-ee shee-mah-soo; Please take us to the art museum.)

- ✔ **Tsukimashita yo.** (tsoo-kee-mah-shee-tah yoh; We're here.)

- ✔ **Otsuri wa kekko desu.** (oh-tsoo-ree wah kehk-kohh deh-soo; Please keep the change.)

Renting a car

If you live in a big city, you may not want to own a **kuruma** (koo-roo-mah; car). Parking space is limited and costly, and insurance is more expensive in the city than in the suburbs. When you want to take a weekend trip, you can **kariru** (kah-ree-roo; rent) a car.

Driving in Japan is tricky. You have to drive on the **hidari gawa** (hee-dah-ree gah-wah; left side) of the **dōro** (dohh-roh; road), and your **handoru** (hahn-doh-roo; steering wheel) is on the **migi gawa** (mee-gee gah-wah; right side) of the car. **Jitensha** (jee-tehn-shah; bicycles) and **hokōsha** (hoh-kohh-shah; pedestrians) always have the right of way on neighborhood streets. The **kōsoku dōro** (kohh-soh-koo dohh-roh; highways) are great, but the **tsūkōryō** (tsooo-kohh-ryohh; tolls) are outrageous.

Conjugate the verb **unten suru** (oon-tehn soo-roo; to drive). If you know how to conjugate the irregular verb **suru** (soo-roo; to do), it's a piece of cake.

Form	*Pronunciation*
unten suru	oon-tehn soo-roo
unten shinai	oon-tehn shee-nah-ee
unten shi	oon-tehn shee
unten shite	oon-tehn shee-teh

If you decide to drive in Japan, go to a **rentakā gaisha** (rehn-tah-kahh gah-ee-shah; rental car company). Their **ryōkin** (ryohh-keen; charges) differ depending on the type of vehicle you choose:

- **yon daburu dī** (yohn dah-boo-ruu deee; four-wheel drive)

- **hai gurēdo sarūn** (hah-ee goo-rehh-doh sah-rooon; luxury car)

- **konpakuto sedan** (kohn-pah-koo-toh seh-dahn; compact sedan)

- **supōtsu taipu** (soo-pohh-tsoo tah-ee-poo; sports car)

- **wagonsha** (wah-gohn-shah; mini-van)

- **supōtsu yūtiritibīkuru** (soo-pohh-tsoo yoo-tee-ree-tee-beee-koo-roo; SUV)

Ask about the car's features:

- ✔ **eakon** (eh-ah-kohn; air conditioning)

- ✔ **manyuaru** (mah-nyoo-ah-roo; stick shift)

- ✔ **ōtomachikku** (ohh-toh-mah-cheek-koo; automatic transmission)

- ✔ **sutereo** (soo-teh-reh-oh; stereo)

Show your **unten menkyoshō** (oon-tehn-mehn-kyoh-shohh; driver's license) to the clerk. Unless you have a Japanese license, you need a **kokusai menkyoshō** (koh-koo-sah-ee mehn-kyoh-shohh; international license) to drive in Japan. Here are some common phrases people use when renting a car:

- ✔ **Kogata no kuruma o karitai-n-desu ga.** (koh-gah-tah noh koo-roo-mah oh kah-ree-tah-een-deh-soo gah; I'd like to rent a small car, but do you have one?)

- ✔ **Kyō kara kinyōbi made tsukai-tai-n-desu.** (kyooo kah-rah keen-yohh-bee mah-deh tsoo-kah-ee-tah-een-deh-soo; I want it today through Friday.)

- ✔ **Mokuyōbi ni kaeshimasu.** (moh-koo-yohh-bee nee kah-eh-shee-mah-soo; I'll return it on Thursday.)

- ✔ **Hoken o kakemasu.** (hoh-kehn oh kah-keh-mah-soo; I'll take the insurance policy.)

Conjugate the verbs **kariru** (kah-ree-roo; to rent) and **kaesu** (kah-eh-soo; to return) — two essential words for visiting a rental-car agency. **Kariru** is a ru-verb, and **kaesu** is a u-verb.

Form	Pronunciation
kariru	kah-ree-roo
karinai	kah-ree-nah-ee
kari	kah-ree
karite	kah-ree-teh

Form	Pronunciation
kaesu	kah-eh-soo
kaesanai	kah-eh-sah-nah-ee
kaeshi	kah-eh-shee
kaeshite	kah-eh-shee-teh

Words to Know

kuruma	koo-roo-mah	car
dōro	dohh-roh	roads
kōsoku dōro	kohh-soh-koo dohh-roh	highways
gasorin sutando	gah-soh-reen soo-tahn-doh	gas station
hoken	hoh-kehn	insurance
rentakā	rehn-tah-kahh	rental car

Dealing with Directions

Don't hesitate to ask for directions in a new town. If you can ask for directions in Japanese, you're ready to go anywhere in Japan.

This section gives you the words and phrases you need to give and receive directions. Is your destination **toī** (tohh-ee; far) or **chikai** (chee-kah-ee; near)?

Asking "where" questions

Suppose you want to go to **shiyakusho** (shee-yah-koo-shoh; city hall). You know it's near the **chikatetsu no eki** (chee-kah-teh-tsoo noh eh-kee; subway station), but you can't see it. What do you do? Check the **jūsho**

(jooo-shoh; address)? Look at a **chizu** (chee-zoo; map)?
Walk around a bit more? If none of these methods
works, ask a kind-looking stranger.

"Where" in Japanese is **doko** (doh-koh). But you can't
just say **doko**. Mention what you're looking for first.
Here are a few places you may be looking for:

- ✔ **Amerika taishikan** (ah-meh-ree-kah tah-ee-shee-kahn; American embassy)

- ✔ **eigakan** (ehh-gah-kahn; movie theater)

- ✔ **gakkō** (gahk-kohh; school)

- ✔ **gasorin sutando** (gah-soh-reen soo-tahn-doh; gas station)

- ✔ **ginkō** (geen-kohh; bank)

- ✔ **hakubutsukan** (hah-koo-boo-tsoo-kahn; museum)

- ✔ **yūbinkyoku** (yooo-been-kyoh-koo; post office)

Put the topic particle **wa** after the place you're
looking for. Then add **doko desu ka** (doh-koh
deh-soo kah; where is) or **doko ni arimasu ka**
(doh-koh nee ah-ree-mah-soo kah; where is it
located). You can use either one:

- ✔ **Byōin wa doko desu ka.** (byohh-een wah doh-koh deh-soo kah; Where is the hospital?)

- ✔ **Ginkō wa doko ni arimasu ka.** (geen-kohh wah doh-koh nee ah-ree-mah-soo kah; Where is the bank located?)

Words to Know

chikai	chee-kah-ee	near
doko	doh-koh	where
tōi	tohh-ee	far
jūsho	jooo-shoh	address

Answering "where" questions

The easiest way to answer a "where" question is to point while saying **Asoko desu** (ah-soh-koh deh-soo; It's over there). Other location words you can use in conjunction with pointing are **koko** (koh-koh) and **soko** (soh-koh). Here's a breakdown for these three words that will make them easy to remember:

Japanese	Pronunciation	Translation	Location
koko	koh-koh	here	near the speaker
soko	soh-koh	there; near you	near the listener, but far from the speaker
asoko	a-soh-koh	over there	far from both the speaker and the listener

If pointing and using these location words doesn't work, use the position phrases listed in Table 9-4.

Table 9-4	Position Phrases	
Position Phrase	**Pronunciation**	**Translation**
hantai (gawa)	hahn-tah-ee (gah-wah)	opposite (side)
hidari (gawa)	hee-dah-ree (gah-wa)	left (side)
mae	mah-eh	front
migi (gawa)	mee-gee (gah-wah)	right (side)
mukai (gawa)	moo-kah-ee (gah-wah)	across the street from
soba	soh-bah	right near
ushiro	oo-shee-roh	behind
aida	ah-ee-dah	between

You can't use one of the phrases in Table 9-4 by itself to describe the location of something. If you say "My house is on the left," no one will understand you. You have to say on the left of what. Use the particle **no** to create a modifier phrase that gives a reference point and place it right before the position phrase. For example, **hakubutsukan no hidari** means "to the left of the museum." You need two reference points for the position **aida** (between). Connect the two points with the particle **to**. For example, **hakubutsukan to eki no aida** means "between the museum and the station."

Use **tonari** (toh-nah-ree; next to) only when you're dealing with two similar things, like two buildings or two seats. If you want to say that the hot-dog vendor is next to the museum, use **yoko** (yoh-koh) instead.

The following phrases put some of these modifiers into context:

- ✔ **Gakkō no ushiro desu.** (gahk-kohh noh oo-shee-roh deh-soo; It's behind the school.)

- ✔ **Gakkō wa byōin no mae desu.** (gahk-kohh wah byohh-een noh mah-eh deh-soo; The school is in front of the hospital.)

- ✔ **Ginkō wa gasorin sutando no tonari desu.** (geen-kohh wah gah-soh-reen soo-tahn-doh noh toh-nah-ree deh-soo; The bank is next to the gas station.)

- ✔ **Yūbinkyoku wa toshokan to shiyakusho no aida desu.** (yooo-been-kyoh-koo wah toh-shoh-kahn toh shee-yah-koo-shoh noh ah-ee-dah deh-soo; The post office is between the library and city hall.)

Specifying how far or near you are to a location is often helpful. The word for "far" is **tōi** (tohh-ee), and the word for "near" is **chikai** (chee-kah-ee). The following examples show you how to use them:

✔ **Chotto tōi desu yo.** (choht-toh tohh-ee deh-soo yoh; It's a bit far.)

✔ **Sugu soko desu.** (soo-goo soh-koh deh-soo; It's right there.)

✔ **Totemo chikai desu.** (toh-teh-moh chee-kah-ee deh-soo; It's very close.)

Giving precise directions

Migi (mee-gee; right) and **hidari** (hee-dah-ree; left) are great, but after you turn 180 degrees or make a couple of lefts and rights, you may get confused. To avoid confusion, specify *cardinal points:*

✔ **kita** (kee-tah; north)

✔ **minami** (mee-nah-mee; south)

✔ **higashi** (hee-gah-shee; east)

✔ **nishi** (nee-shee; west)

✔ **hokusē** (hoh-koo-sehh; northwest)

✔ **hokutō** (hoh-koo-tohh; northeast)

✔ **nansei** (nahn-sehh; southwest)

✔ **nantō** (nahn-tohh; southeast)

Using ordinal numbers

Ordinal number phrases like "the first" and "the second" are essential for pinpointing houses, buildings, intersections, and streets. Remember that quantity phrases like **go-hon** (goh-hohn) and **mit-tsu** (meet-tso) express how many things there are and, depending on the type of the item, you may need a different counter (see Chapter 2). For example, you need the counter **-hon** if you're counting long items like streets, and you use the counter **-tsu** for inanimate objects that don't have a counter of their own.

You convert quantity phrases into ordinal number phrases, which tell you which one in a sequence, by adding **-me** after them. If you're talking about streets,

go-hon (goh-hohn) means "five streets," but **go-hon-me** (goh-hohn-meh) means "the fifth street." If you're talking about intersections, **mit-tsu** (meet-tsoo) means "three intersections," and **mit-tsu-me** (meet-tsoo-meh) means "the third intersection."

Now you're ready to specify at which intersection you should turn. Do you turn at the **hito-tsu-me** (hee-toh-tsoo-meh; first one), **futa-tsu-me** (foo-tah-tsoo-meh; second one), or **mit-tsu-me** (meet-tsoo-meh; third one)? You can also specify which building on the street has a public bathroom.

- ✔ **hito-tsu-me no tatemono** (hee-toh-tsoo-meh noh tah-teh-moh-noh; the first building)

- ✔ **futa-tsu-me no kōsaten** (foo-tah-tsoo-meh noh kohh-sah-tehn; the second intersection)

- ✔ **migi gawa no mit-tsu-me no ie** (mee-gee gah-wah noh meet-tsoo-meh noh ee-eh; the third house on the right-hand side)

- ✔ **yon-hon-me no michi** (yohn-hohn-meh noh mee-chee; the fourth street)

Table 9-5 lists a selection of ordinal numbers.

Table 9-5	Ordinal Numbers		
English	*Tsu-me (Various Items)*	*Hon-me (Long Items)*	*Mai-me (Flat Items)*
1st	hito-tsu-me (hee-toh-tsoo-meh)	ip-pon-me (eep-pohn-meh)	ichi-mai-me (ee-chee-mah-ee-meh)
2nd	futa-tsu-me (foo-tah-tsoo-meh)	ni-hon-me (nee-hohn-meh)	ni-mai-me (nee-mah-ee-meh)
3rd	mit-tsu-me (meet-tsoo-meh)	san-bon-me (sahn-bohn-meh)	san-mai-me (sahn-mah-ee-meh)

(continued)

Table 9-5 *(continued)*

English	Tsu-me (Various Items)	Hon-me (Long Items)	Mai-me (Flat Items)
4th	yot-tsu-me (yoht-tsoo-meh)	yon-hon-me (yohn-hohn-meh)	yon-mai-me (yohn-mah-ee-meh)
5th	itsu-tsu-me (ee-tsoo-tsoo-meh)	go-hon-me (goh-hohn-meh)	go-mai-me (goh-mah-ee-meh)
6th	mut-tsu-me (moot-tsoo-meh)	rop-pon-me (rohp-pohn-meh)	roku-mai-me (roh-koo-mah-ee-meh)
7th	nana-tsu-me (nah-nah-tsoo-meh)	nana-hon-me (nah-nah-hohn-meh)	nana-mai-me (nah-nah-mah-ee-meh)
8th	yat-tsu-me (yaht-tsoo-meh)	hap-pon-me (hahp-pohn-meh)	hachi-mai-me (hah-chee-mah-ee-meh)
9th	kokono-tsu-me (koh-koh-noh-tsoo-meh)	kyū-hon-me (kyooo-hohn-meh)	kyū-mai-me (kyooo-mah-ee-meh)

Specifying how far

You can express distance by specifying the time it takes to get somewhere. Use the counter **-fun** (foon) for minutes. As the following examples show, **-fun** expresses both a point in time and a period of time. **-fun** changes to **-pun** depending on the preceding sound.

✔ **Ima gozen ju-ji jugo-fun desu.** (ee-mah goh-zehn jooo-jee jooo-goh-foon deh-soo; It's 10:15 a.m. now.)

✔ **Uchi kara gakkō made 10-pun desu.** (oo-chee kah-rah gahk-kohh mah-deh joop-poon deh-soo; My school is ten minutes away from my house.)

Use **-jikan** (jee-kahn) for specifying hours. Just add **kan** after the counter **-ji** (jee; o'clock). For some practical examples, see the following list:

- ✔ **Aruite 30-pun desu.** (ah-roo-ee-teh sahn-joop-poon deh-soo; Thirty minutes on foot.)

- ✔ **Kūkō made basu de ni-jikan desu.** (kooo-kohh mah-deh bah-soo deh nee-jee-kahn deh-soo; It is two hours to the airport by bus.)

- ✔ **Koko kara kuruma de go-fun gurai desu.** (koh-koh kah-rah koo-roo-mah deh goh-foon goo-rah-ee deh-soo; It's about five minutes from here by car.)

You can also specify the actual distance:

- ✔ **Eki made ni-kiro desu.** (eh-kee mah-deh nee-kee-roh deh-soo; It's 2 kilometers to the railway station.)

- ✔ **Koko kara ichi-mairu gurai desu.** (koh-koh kah-rah ee-chee mah-ee-roo goo-rah-ee deh-soo; It's about 1 mile from here.)

Asking "how do I get to" questions

Sometimes you have to ask "how do I get to" questions to reach your destination. Ask these questions at a **ryokō annaijo** (ryoh-kohh ahn-nah-ee-jo; tourist bureau), **eki no kippu uriba** (eh-kee noh keep-poo oo-ree-bah; railway-station ticket counter), **gasorin sutando** (gah-soh-reen soo-tahn-doh; gas station), or **hoteru no furonto** (hoh-teh-roo noh foo-rohn-toh; hotel front desk).

To ask a "how do I get to" question, place the question word **dōyatte** (dohh-yaht-teh; how) right after the destination phrase and the particle **wa** (wah), as in the following examples:

- ✔ **Amerika taishikan wa dōyatte iku-n-desu ka.** (ah-meh-ree-kah tah-ee-shee-kahn wah dohh-yaht-teh ee-koon-deh-soo kah; How can I get to the American embassy?)

✔ **Shiyakusho wa dōyatte iku-n-desu ka.** (shee-yah-koo-shoh wah dohh-yaht-teh ee-koon-deh-soo kah; How can I get to city hall?)

Finding out whether you need transportation to get to your destination is a good idea. Ask whether your destination is within walking distance. In this case, you use the verb in the "can" form. (See Chapter 7 for a discussion of "can.")

✔ **Koko kara Akihabara made arukemasu ka.** (koh-koh kah-rah ah-kee-hah-bah-rah mah-deh ah-roo-keh-mah-soo kah; Can I walk to Akihabara from here?)

✔ **Shiyakusho made aruite ikemasu ka.** (shee-yah-koo-shoh mah-deh ah-roo-ee-teh ee-keh-mah-soo *k*ah; Can I get to city hall on foot?)

Conjugate the u-verb **aruku** (ah-roo-koo; to walk). Pay attention to the *k* syllables.

Form	Pronunciation
aruku	ah-roo-koo
arukanai	ah-roo-kah-nah-ee
aruki	ah-roo-kee
aruite	ah-roo-ee-teh

Referring to locations on the street

When giving directions, include several landmarks that the person has to pass to get to his or her destination. Your directions will be more complete if you incorporate the terms in Table 9-6.

Table 9-6	Landmarks	
Landmark	**Pronunciation**	**Translation**
fumikiri	foo-mee-kee-ree	railway crossing
hashi	hah-shee	bridge

Landmark	Pronunciation	Translation
ichiji teishi	ee-chee-jee tehh-shee	stop
kado	kah-doh	corner
kōsaten	kohh-sah-tehn	intersection
michi	mee-chee	road
shingō	sheen-gohh	traffic light
tōri	tohh-ree	street
tsukiatari	tsoo-kee-ah-tah-ree	dead end

There's a subtle difference between **michi** (mee-chee; road) and **tōri** (tohh-ree; street). Both have two functions — to connect locations and to accommodate stores and houses. Although each performs both functions, the emphasis of **michi** is on the connection, and the emphasis of **tōri** is on the accommodation of shops or homes.

You can combine landmarks with the ordinal numbers introduced earlier in this chapter to give pretty specific directions, such as **mittsu-me no shingō** (meet-tsoo-meh noh sheen-gohh; the third traffic light) or **itsu-tsu-me no kado** (ee-tsoo-tsoo-meh noh kah-doh; the fifth corner).

Providing actions with directions

You can't give directions without telling someone how to move — walk, cross, pass, turn, and so on. Check out Table 9-7 for some convenient action words to include in your directions.

Table 9-7	Moving Verbs	
Verb (Dictionary, Negative, Stem, and Te-forms)	**Pronunciation**	**Translation**
aruku [u]	ah-roo-koo	walk
arukanai	ah-roo-kah-nah-ee	
aruki	ah-roo-kee	
aruite	ah-roo-ee-teh	
kudaru [u]	koo-dah-roo	go down
kudaranai	koo-dah-rah-nah-ee	
kudari	koo-dah-ree	
kudatte	koo-daht-teh	
magaru [u]	mah-gah-roo	make a turn
magaranai	mah-gah-rah-nah-ee	
magari	mah-gah-ree	
magatte	mah-gaht-teh	
noboru [u]	noh-boh-roo	go up
noboranai	noh-boh-rah-nah-ee	
nobori	noh-boh-ree	
nobotte	noh-boht-teh	
sugiru [ru]	soo-gee-roo	pass
suginai	soo-gee-nah-ee	
sugi	soo-gee	
sugite	soo-gee-teh	
wataru [u]	wah-tah-roo	cross
wataranai	wah-tah-rah-nah-ee	
watari	wah-tah-ree	
watatte	wah-taht-teh	

Where do you make a turn? What do you cross?
Which street do you take? Specify these locations by
marking them with the particle **o**, directly following
the word for the location or landmark.

- ✔ **kōsaten o magaru** (kohh-sah-tehn oh mah-gah-roo; turn at the intersection)

- ✔ **hashi o wataru** (hah-shee oh wah-tah-roo; cross the bridge)

- ✔ **kono michi o aruku** (koh-noh mee-chee oh ah-roo-koo; walk along this road)

Specify the direction of your movement by marking it
with the particle **ni:**

- ✔ **migi ni magaru** (mee-gee nee mah-gah-roo; make a right turn)

- ✔ **higashi ni iku** (hee-gah-shee nee ee-koo; go east)

Now you're ready to put everything together — where
to make a move, which direction to move in, and how
far to go. Give complete directions:

- ✔ **san-ban-dōri o minami ni iku** (sahn-bahn-dohh-ree oh mee-nah-mee nee ee-koo; go south on Third Street)

- ✔ **go-fun gurai aruku** (goh-foon goo-rah-ee ah-roo-koo; walk about five minutes)

- ✔ **futatsu-me no kado o migi ni magaru** (foo-tah-tsoo-meh noh kah-doh oh mee-gee nee mah-gah-roo; make a right at the second corner)

- ✔ **ginkō o sugiru** (geen-kohh oh soo-gee-roo; pass the bank)

- ✔ **kaidan o noboru** (kah-ee-dahn oh noh-boh-roo; go up the stairs)

- ✔ **kono michi o massugu iku** (koh-noh mee-chee oh mahs-soo-goo ee-koo; go straight on this street)

- ✔ **kōsaten o hidari ni magaru** (kohh-sah-tehn oh hee-dah-ree nee mah-gah-roo; make a left at the intersection)

Chapter 10

Finding a Place to Lay Your Weary Head

● ●

In This Chapter

▶ Finding accommodations

▶ Reserving a room

▶ Arriving at a hotel

▶ Checking out

● ●

Choosing the right **hoteru** (hoh-teh-roo; hotel) can make any trip more enjoyable. Each day of your adventure starts and ends at the hotel. In the morning, a good hotel offers you a refreshing breakfast and, at night, a comfortable bed. Hopefully, the clerks at the **furonto** (foo-rohn-toh; front desk) are kind and helpful.

This chapter goes through the entire process of a hotel stay — choosing the right one, making a reservation, checking in, and checking out. Enjoy your visit!

Getting the Accommodations of Your Choice

Choose **shukuhaku shisetsu** (shoo-koo-hah-koo shee-seh-tsoo; accommodations) according to your needs and budget.

✔ Are you planning a family trip to a resort area near the coast? Get a nice **hoteru** (hoh-teh-roo; hotel) with easy access to the beach.

✔ If you don't want any surprises, you may want to stay at a property owned by a well-known **hoteru chēn** (hoh-teh-roo chehhn; hotel chain).

✔ If you're staying in a sleepy little town for several days, try a **bī ando bī** (beee ahn-doh beee; bed-and-breakfast).

✔ If an extended trip is in your future, you can save some money by staying in a **mōteru** (mohh-teh-roo; motel).

A **hoteru** (hoh-teh-roo; hotel) is a Western-style hotel. You can eat a Western-style **chōshoku** (chohh-shoh-koo; breakfast), sleep on a **beddo** (behd-doh; bed) instead of a futon, and use a Western-style **o-furo** (oh-foo-roh; bath). These familiar amenities may put you at ease, but they don't set off any bells on the new-culture meter.

If you want authentic Japanese-style accommodations, go to a **ryokan** (ryoh-kahn; Japanese-style inn). At the entrance, a **nakai-san** (nah-kah-ee-sahn; maid) in a kimono welcomes you. Enjoy a big **o-furo** (oh-foo-roh; bath) with the other guests and then have a Japanese-style breakfast. When you retire to your room for the evening, dinner is brought right to the living/dining area of your room. You wear a special kimono-like robe, a **yukata** (yoo-kah-tah), while you eat. After dinner, the **futon** (foo-tohn; thin, quilted mattress) is spread out on the **tatami** (tah-tah-mee; straw mat) floor in your bedroom.

A **minshuku** (meen-shoo-koo) is a private home that offers lodging and meals to tourists. All the **minshuku** guests eat their meals together in a big dining room with a **tatami** floor. Guests spread out their own **futon** when they sleep and fold them up again in the morning. It's like visiting a relative's big house in the countryside.

If you're young and your budget is tight, you can stay in a **yūsu hosuteru** (yooo-soo hoh-soo-teh-roo; youth hostel). You have to share a room and/or a bathroom with other travelers and follow the hostel's strict rules, but you can save money for other parts of your trip.

Reserving a Room

Before calling a hotel to **yoyaku suru** (yoh-yah-koo soo-roo; to make a reservation), know how many rooms you need, how long you're staying, and how much you can spend. Then have your **kurejitto kādo** (koo-reh-jeet-toh kahh-doh; credit card) ready and dial the number. If you're already traveling, just walk into the hotel and ask whether they have a room for you.

Japanese doesn't have simple verbs that mean "to plan" or "to make a reservation." To say "to plan" and "to make a reservation," combine the verb **suru** (soo-roo; to do) with a noun — like **keikaku** (kehh-kah-koo; plan) and **yoyaku** (yoh-yah-koo; reservation). **Keikaku suru** means "to plan," and **yoyaku suru** means "to make a reservation." To conjugate these verbs, you simply conjugate the **suru** part (see Chapter 7 for the conjugation). **Suru** is an irregular verb.

Checking out room size

Ask the folks at the front desk about the types of **heya** (heh-yah; rooms) they have.

Following are the words for the types of hotel rooms:

- ✔ **shinguru** (sheen-goo-roo; single)
- ✔ **tsuin** (tsoo-een; twin)

- **semi-daburu** (seh-mee-dah-boo-roo; semi-double/a room with a full-size bed)

- **daburu** (dah-boo-roo; double)

Compare room sizes and prices. Do you want a twin room or a double room? When asking a choice question involving two items, use **dochira** (doh-chee-rah; which one — see Chapter 6 for more on comparisons), as in these examples:

- **Daburu to tsuin to, dochira ga yoroshii desu ka.** (dah-boo-roo toh tsoo-een toh, doh-chee-rah gah yoh-roh-sheee deh-soo kah; We have double and twin rooms. Which one would you like?)

- **Dochira no heya ga hiroi desu ka.** (doh-chee-rah noh heh-yah gah hee-roh-ee deh-soo kah; Which room is bigger?)

- **Dochira ga takai desu ka.** (doh-chee-rah gah tah-kah-ee deh-soo kah; Which one is more expensive?)

Counting the number of guests

Room costs differ depending on the number of people sharing the room. Express the number of people in your party by using the counter **-nin,** but watch out for the irregular "one person" and "two people."

- **hitori** (hee-toh-ree; one person)

- **futari** (foo-tah-ree; two people)

- **san-nin** (sahn-neen; three people)

- **yo-nin** (yoh-neen; four people)

- **go-nin** (goh-neen; five people)

To ask for an extra bed, use the convenient word **mō hitotsu** (mohh hee-toh-tsoo; one more) and request a bed by saying **Beddo o mō hitotsu onegaishimasu** (behd-doh oh mohh hee-toh-tsoo oh-neh-gah-ee shee-mah-soo; One more bed please).

Words to Know

heya	heh-yah	room
nagame	nah-gah-meh	view
dochira	doh-chee-rah	which one (of two)
-nin	neen	counter for people
yoyaku	yoh-yah-koo	reservation

Indicating the length of your stay

Specify how long you want to **tomaru** (toh-mah-roo; to stay). To start with, why don't you conjugate the verb **tomaru**? It's a u-verb.

Form	Pronunciation
tomaru	toh-mah-roo
tomaranai	toh-mah-rah-nah-ee
tomari	toh-mah-ree
tomatte	toh-maht-teh

Use the particles **kara** (kah-rah; from) and **made** (mah-deh; until) to talk about the length of your stay. **Kara** and **made** look like English prepositions, but they follow, not precede, the relevant phrases. For example, "from the 15th" in English is "the 15th from" in Japanese, and "until the 23rd" in English is "the 23rd until" in Japanese. So now you know that **15-nichi kara** (jooo-goh-nee-chee kah-rah) means "from the 15th," and **23-nichi made** (nee-jooo-sahn-nee-chee mah-deh) means "until the 23rd." Take a look at a few examples:

> ✔ **Raishū no getsuyōbi kara mokuyōbi made onegaishimasu.** (rah-ee-shooo noh geh-tsoo-yohh-bee kah-rah moh-koo-yohh-bee mah-deh oh-neh-gah-ee-shee-mah-soo; From Monday to Thursday of next week, please.)

✔ **San-gatsu 15-nichi kara 23-nichi made desu.**
(sahn-gah-tsoo jooo-goh-nee-chee kah-rah nee-jooo-sahn-nee-chee mah-deh deh-soo; I want to stay from March 15 to the 23rd.)

✔ **Kyō kara asatte made tomarimasu.** (kyohh kah-rah ah-saht-teh mah-deh toh-mah-ree-mah-soo; I'll stay from today until the day after tomorrow.)

Use the counter **-haku** (hah-koo) to specify the number of nights you're staying. **-Haku** is the counter for nights spent away from home. Remember to watch out for the **-haku/-paku** alternation. You just have to memorize it.

✔ **ip-paku** (eep-pah-koo; one night)

✔ **ni-haku** (nee-hah-koo; two nights)

✔ **san-paku** (sahn-pah-koo; three nights)

✔ **yon-haku** (yohn-hah-koo; four nights)

✔ **go-haku** (goh-hah-koo; five nights)

✔ **isshūkan** (ees-shooo-kahn, one week)

If you plan to stay a week, say **isshūkan**.

Talking with insiders and outsiders

The distinction between *inside* and *outside* is very important in Japanese. Your choice between a formal speech style or an informal one depends heavily on whether the person you're talking to is your insider or outsider.

The two important words **uchi** (oo-chee; inside) and **soto** (soh-toh; outside) mean not only physical locations, such as inside or outside the house, but also social groupings: *our group* versus *their group*. So the word **uchi** can mean both one's household and one's group. For example, if a hotel clerk says **Uchi wa yasui desu yo** (oo-chee wah yah-soo-ee deh-soo yoh), the phrase doesn't mean "My house doesn't charge much"; it means "Our hotel doesn't charge much."

Comparing costs

Cost is a major criterion when you choose a hotel. Do all the research and **keikaku suru** (kehh-kah-koo soo-roo; plan) carefully.

Making comparisons in Japanese is easy. All you need is the particle **yori** (yoh-ree; than). For example, **Yūsu hosuteru wa yasui desu** (yooo-soo-hoh-soo-teh-roo wah yah-soo-ee deh-soo) means "Youth hostels are cheap." If you want to say "Youth hostels are cheaper than hotels," say **Yūsu hosuteru wa hoteru yori yasui desu** (yooo-soo-hoh-soo-teh-roo wah hoh-teh-roo yoh-ree yah-soo-ee deh-soo).

Keeping track of what's yours with possessive pronouns

When you're traveling, you want to keep track of your **sūtsukēsu** (sooo-tsoo-kehh-soo; suitcases), **handobaggu** (hahn-doh-bagh-goh; handbag), **saifu** (sah-ee-foo; wallet), and **kagi** (kah-gee; keys). If a guy reaches for your **kagi** on a table in the hotel lobby, tell him right away that the keys are yours.

Creating possessive pronouns in Japanese is easy. To say "yours" and "mine," for example, take the words that mean "you" and "I" and add the particle **no** after them:

- ✔ **anata** (ah-nah-tah; you)
- ✔ **anata no** (ah-nah-tah noh; yours)
- ✔ **watashi** (wah-tah-shee; I)
- ✔ **watashi no** (wah-tah-shee-noh; mine)

Piece of cake, right? Now you can say **Watashi no desu** (wah-tah-shee-noh deh-soo; That's mine!) to the guy reaching for your keys.

If you know *yours* and *mine* in Japanese, you already know *your* and *my* because they're exactly the same. **Watashi no desu** (wah-tah-shee-noh deh-soo) means

"That's mine," and **Watashi no kagi desu** (wah-tah-shee noh kah-gee deh-soo) means "That's my key." **Watashi no** means both "mine" and "my." If the phrase is followed by a noun like **kagi**, it means "my;" if it's not followed by a noun, it means "mine." Table 10-1 lists the basic personal pronouns and their ownership counterparts.

Table 10-1   Personal and Possessive Pronouns

Personal Pronoun	Translation	Ownership Word	Translation
watashi (wah-tah-shee)	I/me	watashi no (wah-tah-shee noh)	my/mine
watashi tachi (wah tah-shee tah-chee)	we/us	watashi tachi no (wah-tah-shee tah-chee noh)	our/ours
anata (ah-nah-tah)	you	anata no (ah-nah-tah noh)	your/yours
anata tachi (ah-nah-tah tah-chee)	you plural	anata tachi no (ah-nah-tah tah-chee noh)	your/yours plural
kare (kah-reh)	he/him	kare no (kah-reh noh)	his
kanojo (kah-noh-joh)	she/her	kanojo no (kah-noh-joh noh)	her/hers
karera (kah-reh-rah)	they/them	karera no (kah-reh-rah noh)	their/theirs

Checking In to a Hotel

As soon as you **tsuku** (tsoo-koo; arrive) at a hotel, a **bōi-san** (bohh-ee-sahn; bellhop) helps you with your baggage. (If you're in Japan, you don't need to tip him.)

Conjugate the u-verb **tsuku** (tsoo-koo; to arrive).

Form	Pronunciation
tsuku	tsoo-koo
tsukanai	tsoo-kah-nah-ee
tsuki	tsoo-kee
tsuite	tsoo-ee-teh

Go to the **furonto** (foo-rohn-toh; front desk). If you don't have a reservation, ask them whether they have an **akibeya** (ah-kee-beh-yah; vacancy). You can say **Akibeya wa arimasu ka** (ah-kee-beh-yah wah ah-ree-mah-soo kah; Any vacancies?).

If you have a reservation or the hotel has a vacancy, **chekku-in suru** (chehk-koo-een soo-roo; check in). Hotel clerks speak very politely. In Japan, a hotel clerk addresses you with your name and **-sama** (sah-mah; Mr./Ms.), which is the super-polite, businesslike version of **-san** (sahn).

The clerk will probably give you a **yōshi** (yohh-shee; form). Write your **namae** (nah-mah-eh; name), **jūsho** (jooo-shoh; address), and **denwa-bangō** (dehn-wah-bahn-gohh; telephone number) on it. If the clerk asks, show your **pasupōto** (pah-soo-pohh-toh; passport). Finally, get a **kagi** (kah-gee; key) for your **heya** (heh-yah; room).

Which floor is your room on? Is it on the **nana-kai** (nah-nah-kah-ee; seventh floor) or on the **37-kai** (sahn-jooo-nah-nah-kah-ee; 37th floor)? Specify your floor by using a numeral plus the counter **-kai**. (For more on Japanese counters, see Chapter 2. For more on numbers, see Chapter 3.)

Which room is yours? Refer to your room by using a numeral plus the counter **-gōshitsu** (gohh-shee-tsoo).

For example, is it **502-gōshitsu** (goh-hyah-koo-nee-gohh-shee-tsoo; room 502) or **2502-gōshitsu** (nee-sehn-goh-hyah-koo-nee-gohh-shee-tsoo; room 2502)?

When you check in, you may want to ask where the parking garage is, whether the hotel has room service, and how to get a wake-up call. You may want to request **kurīningu sābisu** (koo-reee-neen-goo sahh-bee-soo; laundry service) or use the hotel **kinko** (keen-koh; safe) to store your valuables. Ask your questions when you check in so that you can **neru** (neh-roo; sleep) well. The following phrases may come in handy:

- ✔ **Chekku-auto wa nan-ji desu ka.** (chehk-koo-ah-oo-toh wah nahn-jee deh-soo kah; When is check-out time?)

- ✔ **Chōshoku wa tsuite imasu ka.** (chohh-shoh-koo wah tsoo-ee-teh ee-mah-soo kah; Is breakfast included?)

- ✔ **Chūshajō wa doko desu ka.** (chooo-shah-johh wah doh-koh deh-soo kah; Where is the parking garage?)

- ✔ **Watashi ni dengon wa arimasen ka.** (wah-tah-shee nee dehn-gohn wah ah-ree-mah-sehn kah; Are there any messages for me?)

- ✔ **Rūmu sābisu wa arimasu ka.** (rooo-moo sahh-bee-soo wah ah-ree-mah-soo kah; Do you offer room service?)

- ✔ **Ashita no roku-ji ni mōningu kōru o onegaishi-masu.** (ah-shee-tah noh roh-koo-jee nee mohh-neen-goo kohh-roo oh oh-neh-gah-ee-shee-mah-soo; Give me a wake-up call at 6:00 tomorrow, please.)

Conjugate the ru-verb **neru** (neh-roo; to sleep).

Form	Pronunciation
neru	neh-roo
nenai	neh-nah-ee
ne	neh
nete	neh-teh

Words to Know

tsuku [u]	tsoo-koo	to arrive
furonto	foo-rohn-toh	front desk
chekku-in	chehk-koo-een	check in
-gōshitsu	gohh-shee-tsoo	counter for room number
kagi	kah-gee	key
mōningu kōru	mohh-neen-goo kohh-roo	wake-up call
rūmu sābisu	rooo-moo sahh-bee-soo	room service
neru	neh-roo	to sleep

Checking Out of a Hotel

It's **chekku-auto** (chehk-koo-ah-oo-toh; check out) time! Pack up your stuff and don't **wasureru** (wah-soo-reh-roo; forget) anything in your room. Go to the **furonto** (foo-rohn-toh; front desk) to **chekku-auto** and pay your bill. You may see some additional charges on your bill:

- ✔ **denwaryō** (dehn-wah-ryohh; telephone usage charge)
- ✔ **inshokuryō** (een-shoh-koo-ryohh; food and drink charge)
- ✔ **kurūningudai** (koo-reee-neen-goo-dah-ee; laundry charge)
- ✔ **zeikin** (zehh-keen; tax)

If you need further assistance from the hotel staff after you check out, just ask

- ✔ **Go-ji made nimotsu o azukatte kudasai.** (goh-jee mah-deh nee-moh-tsoo oh ah-zoo-kaht-teh koo-dah-sah-ee; Please keep my baggage here until 5:00.)

- ✔ **Ryōshusho o kudasai.** (ryohh-shooo-shoh oh koo-dah-sah-ee; Please give me the receipt.)

- ✔ **Takushī o yonde kudasai.** (tah-koo-sheee oh yohn-deh koo-dah-sah-ee; Please call a taxi.)

If the clerks can accommodate your request, they'll say **kekkō desu** (kehk-kohh deh-soo; it's good). **Kekkō desu** is the polite version of **ii desu** (eee deh-soo; it's good).

Be careful. Both **kekkō desu** and **ii desu** can mean either "that's fine" or "no thank you," depending on the situation. If a clerk says **kekkō desu** in response to a request, it means "that's fine." But if someone says **kekkō desu** right after you offer him or her a drink, it means "no thank you."

By adding **masen ka** (mah-sehn kah) to the end of a request like **tabete kudasai** (tah-beh-teh koo-dah-sah-ee; eat please), you can make the request sound softer and more polite. For example, **tabete kudasai masen ka** sounds much more polite than **tabete kudasai**. **Masen** is just a polite suffix in the negative form, and **ka** is the question parti-cle. It means something like "Wouldn't you?" or "Would you mind?" Use **masen ka** when you ask a favor of a hotel clerk.

Chapter 11

Dealing with Emergencies

. . . .

In This Chapter

▶ Calling for help

▶ Contacting the police

▶ Finding legal assistance

▶ Locating a doctor

. . . .

*K*nowing what to do in case an illness, injury, or emergency pops up is important. This chapter provides you with the confidence and the vocabulary to act wisely when faced with an emergency.

Shouting out for Help

When you're in a panic, making even the slightest of sounds may be difficult, but use your stomach power and shout it out! But what should you shout? Use the following phrases to call for help:

▶ **Abunai!** (ah-boo-nah-ee; Watch out!)

▶ **Dareka!** (dah-reh-kah; Someone help!)

▶ **Tasukete!** (tah-soo-keh-teh; Help me!)

▶ **Dorobō!** (doh-roh-bohh; A thief!)

▶ **Kaji!** (kah-jee; Fire!)

▶ **Kēsatsu!** (kehh-sah-tsoo; Police!)

Tasukete is the te-form of the verb **tasukeru** (tah-soo-keh-roo; to help). It's the product of omitting **kudasai** (koo-dah-sah-ee) from the sentence **Tasukete kudasai** (tah-soo-keh-teh koo-dah-sah-ee; Please help me). Remember that you express a request by using a verb in the te-form plus **kudasai**. **Kudasai** is a sort of helping verb. In an informal situation or in an emergency, you can omit it.

Following is the conjugation of the verb **tasukeru** (tah-soo-keh-roo; to help), a ru-verb. Use its te-form **tasukete** to call for help.

Form	Pronunciation
tasukeru	tah-soo-keh-roo
tasukenai	tah-soo-keh-nah-ee
tasuke	tah-soo-keh
tasukete	tah-soo-keh-teh

If you see someone who appears to be having a problem, don't scream. Just ask

✔ **Daijōbu desu ka.** (dah-ee-johh-boo deh-soo kah; Are you all right?)

✔ **Dōshita-n-desu ka.** (dohh-shee-tahn-deh-soo kah; What happened?)

To call for help, knowing the u-verb **yobu** (yoh-boo; to call) helps. It means "to call" in a general sense, not necessarily by telephone. Practice conjugating the verb **yobu**. The *b* syllables are fun to say, but make sure that you end the te-form with **-nde**.

Form	Pronunciation
yobu	yoh-boo
yobanai	yoh-bah-nah-ee
yobi	yoh-bee
yonde	yohn-deh

The best way to express your helpful intentions is to ask a question that ends in **-mashō ka** (mah-shohh kah; shall I?). **-Mashō ka** follows a verb in the stem form. The stem form of **yobu** (yoh-boo; to call) is **yobi** (yoh-bee); therefore, **Kēsatsu o yobimashō ka** (kehh-sah-tsoo oh yoh-bee-mah-shohh kah) means "Shall I call the police?"

If you can't handle a situation alone, ask the people around you to help out, too. To make this request, use a verb in the te-form and add **kudasai** (koo-dah-sah-ee), as discussed earlier in this section. Here are a few examples using the verbs **suru** and **yomu**:

- ✔ **Kēsatsu ni denwa shite kudasai.** (kehh-sah-tsoo nee dehn-wah shee-teh koo-dah-sah-ee; Phone the police please.)

- ✔ **Kyūkyūsha o yonde kudasai.** (kyooo-kyooo-shah oh yohn-deh koo-dah-sah-ee; Call an ambulance please.)

- ✔ **Shōbōsho ni denwa shite kudasai.** (shohh-bohh-shoh nee dehn-wah shee-teh koo-dah-sah-ee; Please phone the fire department.)

Words to Know

Daijōbu desu ka.	dah-ee-johh-boo deh-soo kah	Are you all right?
dorobō	doh-roh-bohh	thief
kaji	kah-jee	fire
kēsatsu	kehh-sah-tsoo	police

continued

Words to Know (continued)

kyūkyūsha	kyooo-kyooo-shah	ambulance
shōbōsho	shohh-bohh-shoh	fire department
tasukeru [ru]	tah-soo-keh-roo	to help
tasukete	tah-soo-keh-teh	help me
yobu [u]	yoh-boo	to call for

Calling the Police

The police emergency number in Japan is 110. The Japanese call it **110-ban** (hyah-koo-tohh-bahn). Yes, they usually say **hyakutō-ban** (hyah-koo-tohh-bahn) rather than **hyakujū-ban** (hyah-koo-jooo-bahn) — it's just one of those things. The number for an accident or fire is **119-ban** (hyah-koo-jooo-kyooo-bahn). When you call an emergency number, remain calm and tell the dispatcher where you are. Then explain what happened.

Reporting an accident to the police

If you see a **jiko** (jee-koh; accident), report it to the **kēsatsu** (kehh-sah-tsoo; police). The verb you need is **aru** (ah-roo; to exist). When you call the police, use the past tense to report the problem — "There was an accident." And remember to use the polite/neutral style when you talk to a police officer.

So you need to conjugate **aru** in the polite past tense form, **arimashita** (ah-ree-mah-shee-tah). Here are a couple of examples:

✔ **Jiko ga arimashita.** (jee-koh gah ah-ree-mah-shee-tah; There was an accident.)

✔ **Takada-chō de jiko ga arimashita.** (tah-kah-dah-chohh deh jee-koh gah ah-ree-mah-shee-tah; There was an accident in Takada Town.)

I hope you don't **okosu** (oh-koh-soo; cause) an accident, and I don't want you to **au** (ah-oo; be involved in) one, either. When you use the verb **au**, mark **jiko** with the particle **ni**, as in **jiko ni au** (jee-koh nee ah-oo; to be involved in an accident). The polite past tense forms of **okosu** and **au** are **okoshimashita** and **aimashita**, as in these examples:

✔ **Hidoi jiko ni aimashita.** (hee-doh-ee jee-koo nee ah-ee-mah-shee-tah; I was involved in a terrible accident.)

✔ **Kinō otōto ga jiko o okoshimashita.** (kee-nohh oh-tohh-toh gah jee-koh oh oh-koh-shee-mah-shee-tah; My brother caused an accident yesterday.)

Conjugate the u-verb **au** (ah-oo; to be involved in). Watch out for the *w* sound in the negative form.

Form	Pronunciation
au	ah-oo
awanai	ah-wah-nah-ee
ai	a-ee
atte	aht-teh

Now conjugate the u-verb **okosu** (o-koh-soo; to cause). Create **s/sh**-syllables.

Form	Pronunciation
okosu	o-koh-soo
okosanai	oh-koh-sah-nah-ee
okoshi	oh-koh-shee
okoshite	oh-koh-shee-teh

Specifying the nature of an accident is often necessary so that the people responding know what to expect.

The following list gives you an idea of some of the types of **jiko** (jee-koh; accidents) that you may encounter:

- **kōtsū jiko** (kohh-tsoo jee-koh; traffic accident)
- **jidōsha jiko** (jee-dohh-shah jee-koh; car accident)
- **kaji** (kah-jee; fire)
- **kega** (keh-gah; injury)

To avoid future legal complications after an accident, call the **kēsatsu** (kehh-sah-tsoo; police). Tell them where you are and **matsu** (mah-tsoo; wait for) the **kēsatsukan** (kehh-sah-tsoo-kahn; police officer) to arrive. To tell the police how to find you, use the location and direction words listed in Chapter 9.

Here's the conjugation of the u-verb **matsu** (mah-tsoo; to wait).

Form	Pronunciation
matsu	mah-tsoo
matanai	mah-tah-nah-ee
machi	mah-chee
matte	maht-teh

Words to Know

au [u]	ah-oo	to encounter
jiko	jee-koh	accident
jidosha jiko	jee-dohh-shah jee-koh	car accident
kēsatsukan	kehh-sah-tsoo-kahn	police officer
matsu [u]	mah-tsoo	to wait
okosu [u]	oh-koh-soo	to cause

Finding the lost and found

Hotels, airlines, and taxi companies have lost-and-found departments that contain countless umbrellas, wallets, cameras, watches, jackets, and so on. If you lose your **handobaggu** (hahn-doh-bahg-goo; handbag), **saifu** (sah-ee-foo; wallet), or **sūtsukēsu** (sooo-tsoo-kehh-soo; suitcase), tell the authorities where you lost it and what it looks like. (Use the words that describe colors and sizes from Chapter 6.) And think about what was in it:

- ✔ **genkin** (gehn-keen; cash)
- ✔ **kurejitto kādo** (koo-reh-jeeht-toh kahh-doh; credit cards)
- ✔ **kagi** (kah-gee; keys)
- ✔ **pasupōto** (pah-soo-pohh-toh; passport)
- ✔ **unten menkyoshō** (oon-tehn mehn-kyoh-shohh; driver's license)

To describe the contents of your bag or wallet, use the phrase **haitte iru** (hah-eet-teh ee-roo; to be in it). **Haitte** is the te-form of the verb **hairu** (hah-ee-roo; to be placed in somewhere).

Conjugate the u-verb **hairu**. It also means "to enter" in some contexts.

Form	Pronunciation
hairu	hah-ee-roo
hairanai	hah-ee-rah-nah-ee
hairi	hah-ee-ree
haitte	hah-eet-teh

If you add the verb **iru** (ee-roo; to exist) after another verb in the te-form, you're talking about a state of being. For example, **haitte iru** (hah-eet-teh ee-roo) is the state after something entered — it means "Something is in it." For example, **Genkin ga haitte iru** (gehn-keehn gah hah-eet-teh ee-roo) means "Some cash is in it." In a polite/neutral context, say **Genkin ga haitte imasu** (gehn-keen gah hah-eet-teh ee-mah-soo).

If you have more than one item in your bag, list everything by using the particle **to** (toh). Simply place the particle **to** after each item except the last one.

> ✔ **Saifu to pasupōto ga haitte imasu.** (sah-ee-foo toh pah-soo-pohh-toh gah hah-eet-teh ee-mah-soo; My wallet and passport are in it.)
>
> ✔ **Genkin to kurejitto kādo to shashin ga haitte imasu.** (gehn-keen toh koo-reh-jeet-toh kahh-doh toh shah-sheen gah hah-eet-teh ee-mah-soo; Some cash, a credit card, and a photo are in it.)
>
> ✔ **Shashin ga haitte imasu.** (shah-sheen gah hah-eet-teh ee-mah-soo; A photo is in it.)

Conjugate the two important verbs in this section — **nakusu** (nah-koo-soo; to lose) and **mitsukaru** (mee-tsoo-kah-roo; to be found); both are u-verbs.

Form	*Pronunciation*
nakusu	nah-koo-soo
nakusanai	nah-koo-sah-nah-ee
nakushi	nah-koo-shee
nakushite	nah-koo-shee-teh

Form	*Pronunciation*
mitsukaru	mee-tsoo-kah-roo
mitsukaranai	mee-tsoo-kah-rah-nah-ee
mitsukari	mee-tsoo-kah-ree
mitsukatte	mee-tsoo-kaht-teh

If you lose something in a store, airport, or train station, listen for an announcement. If you're paged over the public-address system, it's a good sign. An announcement states your name and **o-koshi kudasai** (oh-koh-shee koo-dah-sah-ee), which is a super-polite, businesslike phrase that means "please come." This phrase uses the stem form — **koshi** — of the verb **kosu** (koh-soo), which means "to pass," "to move," or "to come," depending on the context. In this case, it obviously means "to come."

Getting Legal Help

If you find that you need legal assistance in Japan, you can always **hanasu** (hah-nah-soo; talk) to a **bengoshi** (behn-goh-shee; lawyer). (The u-verb **hanasu** is conjugated below.) It's also a good idea to **renraku suru** (rehn-rah-koo soo-roo; contact) your country's consulate if you run into trouble.

Form	*Pronunciation*
hanasu	hah-nah-soo
hanasanai	hah-nah-sah-nah-ee
hanashi	hah-nah-shee
hanashite	hah-nah-shee-teh

You may find these sentences helpful:

- ✔ **Amerika ryōjikan ni renraku shite kudasai.** (ah-meh-ree-kah ryohh-jee-kahn nee rehn-rah-koo shee-teh koo-dah-sah-ee; Please contact the American consulate.)
- ✔ **Bengoshi o yonde kudasai.** (behn-goh-shee oh yohn-deh koo-dah-sah-ee; Please call a lawyer.)
- ✔ **Watashi no bengoshi ni hanashite kudasai.** (wah-tah-shee noh behn-goh-shee nee hah-nah-shee-teh koo-dah-sah-ee; Please talk to my lawyer.)

Words to Know

hanasu [u]	hah-nah-soo	to talk
bengoshi	behn-goh-shee	lawyer
ryōjikan	ryohh-jee-kahn	consulate

Getting Medical Help

It's hard enough to understand doctor-talk in your own language, let alone in a foreign one. If you get sick in Japan, you may want to prepare for your visit to the **o-isha-san** (oh-ee-shah-sahn; doctor) by going over the keywords for your **shōjō** (shohh-johh; symptoms) and for the **kensa** (kehn-sah; tests), **shindan** (sheen-dahn; diagnoses), **kusuri** (koo-soo-ree; medications), and **chiryō** (chee-ryohh; treatments) you may receive.

Looking for a doctor

If you have a medical emergency, go to the **kyūkyū byoin** (kyooo-kyooo byohh-een; emergency hospital) and don't forget to bring your ID and insurance cards. If the situation is not an emergency, choose a **byōin** (byohh-een; hospital/doctor's office) and see a **senmon-i** (sehn-mohn-ee; medical specialist), such as a

- **ganka-i** (gahn-kah-ee; ophthalmologist)
- **haisha** (hah-ee-shah; dentist)
- **hifuka-i** (hee-foo-kah-ee; dermatologist)
- **naika-i** (nah-ee-kah-ee; internist)
- **sanfujinka-i** (sahn-foo-jeen-kah-ee; obstetrician and gynecologist)
- **sēkē geka-i** (sehh-kehh geh-kah-ee; orthopedist)
- **shōnika-i** (shohh-nee-kah-ee; pediatrician)

O-isha-san ni iku (oh-ee-shah-sahn nee ee-koo) literally means "to go to a doctor," but it actually means "to go *see* a doctor." Use the verb **iku** (ee-koo; to go) when you go see any kind of doctor.

Words to Know

byōin	byohh-een	hospital
haisha	hah-ee-shah	dentist
naika	nah-ee-kah	internal medicine
naika-i	nah-ee-kah-ee	internist
o-isha-san	oh-ee-shah-sahn	medical doctors (in general)
senmon-i	sehn-mohn-ee	medical specialist

Pointing at your body parts

To explain your **shōjō** (shohh-johh; symptoms) to the doctor, specify *where* it hurts. Table 11-1 gives the Japanese words for body parts.

Table 11-1	Parts of the Body	
Body Part	*Pronunciation*	*Translation*
ashi	ah-shee	foot/leg
atama	ah-tah-mah	head
hiza	hee-zah	knee
kata	kah-tah	shoulder
koshi	koh-shee	hip
kubi	koo-bee	neck
kuchi	koo-chee	mouth
me	meh	eyes

(continued)

Table 11-1 *(continued)*

Body Part	Pronunciation	Translation
mimi	mee-mee	ears
mune	moo-neh	chest
nodo	noh-doh	throat
onaka	oh-nah-kah	belly
senaka	seh-nah-kah	back
te	teh	hand/arm
ude	oo-deh	arm

If some part of your body hurts, say the part that hurts, plus **ga** (gah), plus **itai** (ee-tah-ee) or **itai-n-desu** (ee-tah-een-deh-soo). By adding **-n-desu,** you sound polite and receptive to the response. **Itai** (ee-tah-ee) is an adjective meaning "painful." **Itai** is also what the Japanese say for "ouch." So **atama ga itai** basically means "head is ouch" — in other words, "I have a headache."

If more than one part hurts, list all the parts by using the particle **to** (toh) as a type of verbal comma and a stand-in for "and." Place **to** after each body part except the last one, as in the following examples:

- ✔ **Kata to kubi ga totemo itai-n-desu.** (kah-tah toh koo-bee gah toh-teh-moh ee-tah-een-deh-soo; My shoulder and neck hurt a lot.)

- ✔ **Kata to koshi to kubi ga itai-n-desu.** (kah-tah toh koh-shee toh koo-bee gah ee-tah-een-deh-soo; My shoulder, back, and neck hurt.)

Complaining about your discomfort

To get the right diagnosis, you need to explain your symptoms to the doctor. Find your symptoms in Table 11-2.

Table 11-2	Suffering from Symptoms	
Symptom	**Pronunciation**	**Translation**
geri o shite iru	geh-ree oh shee-teh ee-roo	to have diarrhea
hakike ga suru	hah-kee-keh gah soo-roo	to have nausea
hana ga tsumatte iru	hah-nah gah tsoo-maht-teh ee-roo	to have a stuffy nose
hanamizu ga deru	hah-nah-mee-zoo gah deh-roo	to have a runny nose
kushami ga deru	koo-shah-mee gah deh-roo	to sneeze
me ga kayui	meh gah kah-yoo-ee	to have itchy eyes
netsu ga aru	neh-tsoo gah ah-roo	to have a fever
nodo ga itai	noh-doh gah ee-tah-ee	to have a sore throat
seki ga deru	seh-kee gah deh-roo	to cough
zutsū ga suru	zoo-tsooo gah soo-roo	to have a headache
zē zē suru	zehh zehh soo-roo	to wheeze

Getting a diagnosis

A doctor can usually diagnose a minor cold or the flu just by talking with you, but sometimes you have to have tests done. A few tests and procedures that a doctor may recommend are

- **chōonpa** (chohh-ohn-pah; sonogram)
- **ketsueki kensa** (keh-tsoo-eh-kee kehn-sah; blood test)

✔ **nyō kensa** (nyohh kehn-sah; urine test)

✔ **rentogen** (rehn-toh-gehn; X-ray)

Possible diagnoses include

✔ **haien** (hah-ee-ehn; pneumonia)

✔ **infuruenza** (een-foo-roo-ehn-zah; influenza)

✔ **kansetsuen** (kahn-seh-tsoo-ehn; arthritis)

✔ **kaze** (kah-zeh; cold)

✔ **kossetsu** (kohs-seh-tsoo; broken bone)

✔ **nenza** (nehn-zah; sprain)

✔ **shokuchūdoku** (shoh-koo-chooo-doh-koo; food poisoning)

Getting treatment

Your doctor may give you some **kusuri** (koo-soo-ree; medication) to make you feel better:

✔ **kōsē busshitsu** (kohh-sehh boos-shee-tsoo; antibiotics)

✔ **asupirin** (ah-soo-poo-reen; asprin)

✔ **itamidome** (ee-tah-mee-doh-meh; pain reliever)

✔ **genetsuzai** (geh-neh-tsoo-zah-ee; fever reducer)

✔ **sekidome** (seh-kee-doh-meh; cough suppressant)

If you have an injury, you may come home with one of these items:

✔ **gipusu** (gee-poo-soo; cast)

✔ **hōtai** (hohh-tah-ee; bandage)

✔ **matsubazue** (mah-tsoo-bah-zoo-eh; crutches)

Chapter 12

Ten Favorite Japanese Expressions

• •

Yatta (I did it!)

Say **yatta** (yaht-tah) when you accomplish something big or receive a great opportunity. Passing a difficult test, getting the job you wanted, or winning the lottery all qualify as **yatta** material.

Hontō (Really?)

Say **hontō** (hohn-tohh) to confirm what you just heard. Suppose your colleague tells you that she's marrying your boss. Respond to the news by saying **hontō.** You can use **hontō** in a lot of situations because unbelievable things happen every day.

Ā, sō desu ka (Really?)

Say **ā, sō desu ka** (ahh, sohh deh-soo kah) every time your conversational partner provides a new piece of information. Be sure to nod as you say this expression. If you talk casually with a Japanese person, you may use this phrase 200 times in an hour.

Mochiron (Of course!)

Use this adverb when you're 100 percent confident in your opinion. If you were a married man, how would you answer this question from your wife: "Would you marry me if you had a chance to do it all over again?" Don't think about it; just say **mochiron** (moh-chee-rohn).

Ā, yokatta (Oh, good)

Say **ā, yokatta** (ahh, yoh-kaht-tah) every time you feel like saying "What a relief" or "Oh, good." If you're a worrier, you may say it ten times a day.

Zenzen (Not at all)

Zenzen (zehn-zehn) is the phrase of denial. Suppose someone asks you, "Am I disturbing you?" If she isn't bothering you, say **zenzen** and shake your head.

Nani (What?)

Say **nani** (nah-nee) when you don't hear or understand what the other person said. You can also say **nani** when you can't believe or don't like what you hear.

Dōshiyō (What shall I do?)

Say **dōshiyō** (dohh-shee-yohh) when you're in a panic and have no idea what to do. You can repeat it over and over while you try to think of a solution.

Ā, bikkurishita (What a surprise!)

Say **ā, bikkurishita** (ahh, beek-koo-ree-shee-tah) when you're very surprised.

Yappari (I knew it would happen)

Sometimes you have a vague suspicion that some-thing will happen, and then it actually happens. At times like that, say **yappari** (yahp-pah-ree).

Chapter 13

Ten Phrases That Make You Sound Like a Local

* *

Enryo shinaide (Don't be shy)

Japanese guests often refuse food or drink offers at least once. If you're the host, say **enryo shinaide** (ehn-ryoh shee-nah-ee-deh).

Mottainai (What a waste/It's too good)

Say **mottainai** (moht-tah-ee-nah-ee) to object to waste. You can also say it if someone lacks a true appreciation for something valuable.

Osakini (Pardon me, but I'm leaving now)

When you have to leave a gathering early, say **osakini** (oh-sah-kee-nee; literally means earlier) to display your thoughtfulness for others.

Sasuga (I'm impressed by you, as usual)

Sasuga (sah-soo-gah) literally means "as might have been expected," but it's commonly used as a compliment. If a friend wins a competition, say **sasuga**.

Gambatte (Try your best!)

The Japanese believe that the effort is more important than the result. If a friend's going to take an important exam, say **gambatte** (gahm-baht-teh) to her.

Shōganai (There's no choice/There's nothing that can be done)

When you're in a jam and none of the possible solutions will work well, choose one and say **shōganai** (shohh-gah-nah-ee), which shows that you've resigned yourself to the situation.

Okage-sama de (Luckily/Thanks to you)

If someone asks **ogenki desu ka** (oh-gehn-kee deh-soo kah; How are you?), answer with the modest **okage-sama de** (oh-kah-geh-sah-mah de) rather than **genki desu** (gehn-kee deh-soo; I'm fine). The original meaning is that your well-being is due to God and others, including the person you're talking to.

Gokurō-sama (Thank you for your trouble)

If you're the boss, say **gokurō-sama** (goh-koo-rohh-sah-mah) to each of your workers when they say good-bye to you at the end of the day.

Yoroshiku (Pleased to meet you/I appreciate your helping me)

You can say **yoroshiku** (yoh-roh-shee-koo) when you first meet someone, as in you're pleased to meet him. You can also say it after asking a favor of someone, in which case it means "I appreciate your helping me."

Taihen desu ne (That's tough)

Use this phrase to show sympathy, such as when your friend tells you about her difficulties.

Index